MEGALOPOLIS

MEGALOPOLIS

CONTEMPORARY CULTURAL SENSIBILITIES

CELESTE OLALQUIAGA

UNIVERSITY OF MINNESOTA PRESS
MINNEAPOLIS ◆ OXFORD

Published by the University of Minnesota Press
2037 University Avenue Southeast, Minneapolis, MN 55414
Printed in the United States of America on acid-free paper

Library of Congress Cataloging-in-Publication Data

Olalquiaga, Celeste.
  Megalopolis : contemporary cultural sensibilities / Celeste Olalquiaga.
     p.   cm.
  Includes bibliographical references and index.
  ISBN 0-8166-1998-0 (hc)—ISBN 0-8166-1999-9 (pb)
    1. Postmodernism—Social aspects.   2. Popular culture.   3. City and town life.
4. Technology—Social aspects.   I. Title.
HM73.043   1992
306.4—dc20   91-12383
                                                                              CIP

A CIP catalog record for this book is available from the British Library.

The University of Minnesota is an
equal-opportunity educator and employer.

to my friends

Ithaca has given you the beautiful voyage.
Konstantin Kavafis, 1911

Contents

Prologue   xi

One   Reach Out and Touch Someone   1

Psychasthenia and the Loss of Spatial Boundaries—Obsessive Compulsive Repetition: Simulation and Pornography—The Organic/Technological Interface—Struggling over the Vanishing Body

Two   Lost in Space   19

The Allegorical Compensation for Cultural Anxiety—Progressing toward a Future in Ruins—Science Fiction; or, Fearing the Body Snatchers—The Space Age as a Parodic Souvenir

Three   Holy Kitschen: Collecting Religious Junk from the Street   36

Religious Iconography as Kitsch: Developing a Vicarious Sensibility—Fourteenth Street and First-Degree Kitsch—Little Rickie and Second-Degree Kitsch—Third-Degree Kitsch and the Advantages of Recycling

Four   *Nature Morte*   56

Melancholic Sensibility and the Scenification of Death—
Contra Natura: Physical Aberration as a Memento Mori—A
Culturescape Made of Old Images, Junk, and Debris—
Fake Scientific Exhibits and the Parody of Systematic
Methodologies

Five   Tupinicópolis: The City of Retrofuturistic Indians   75

The Latinization of the United States—Nostalgia as a
Cultural Hindrance—Latin American Postindustrial Pop—
Reinventing Roles in Postcolonial Culture

Epilogue   93

Notes   95

Index   107

Prologue

Postmodernism lives. Legions of detractors and years of intellectual debate have done nothing to arrest its expansion or reduce its impact, and scores of usurpers have failed miserably in stultifying its scope. Despite or because of being profanely ambivalent and ambiguous, rejoicing in consumption and celebrating obsessions, ignoring consistency and avoiding stability, favoring illusions and pleasure, postmodernism is the only possible contemporary answer to a century worn out by the rise and fall of modern ideologies, the pervasion of capitalism, and an unprecedented sense of personal responsibility and individual impotence.

Whether one likes it or not, postmodernism is a state of things. It is primarily determined by an extremely rapid and freewheeling exchange to which most responses are faltering, impulsive, and contradictory. What is at stake is the very constitution of being—the ways we perceive ourselves and others, the modes of experience that are available to us, the women and men whose sensibilities are shaped by urban exposure.

At the risk of being thrown to the lions, I admit that in general I find the debate about postmodernism monotonous, verbose, and self-referential. It is either reduced exclusively to art or caught up in a web of academic disquisitions, neither of which is of much interest to people outside those worlds. Furthermore, the postmodern debate is often tied into a right-or-wrong kind of argumentation that drains post-modernism of two of its most important features: versatility and the emptying of hierarchies. Consequently, instead of discussing in this prologue the main literature about postmodernism, I will look at those texts that have shaped *Megalopolis* in one way or another.

Walter Benjamin, a lyrical critic in the age of modern capitalism, is perhaps the most influential thinker for the kind of cultural study practiced here. Benjamin's work is fundamental for any complex reading of city life, and his splendid writing is a continuous source of inspiration. Benjamin's understanding of allegory and melancholy, as well as his privileging of random looking, fragmentary insights, and imagery, together with a nonjudgmental attitude toward mass culture, anticipated the postmodern gaze.[1]

One could say, following Deleuze and Guattari, that Benjamin's method is "rhyzomatic" in that it abandons dualism and linear thinking in favor of multiple associations at different semiotic levels.[2] In this way Benjamin can, for example, map the conflicts of a nascent modernity through Baudelaire's poetry or describe the dramatic reconstitution of perception in the distracted flounderings of that exemplary urbanite, the *flaneur,* whose main pleasure was to get lost in the crowds so as to observe the world in peaceful anonymity. Benjamin moves swiftly between philosophy and street signs, personal memories and literary tropes, inaugurating a way of looking at things whose full recognition is still due, as the academic reticence toward interdisciplinary cultural studies clearly shows.

At the heart of this reticence lies a deeply rooted belief that culture, unless it is manifested in one of the liberal arts, is not a proper object of intellectual attention. At best, cultural phenomena qualify for statistical proof of the determining power of "real" discourses (i.e., for progressive thought, the intricate web of class, race, and gender) whose autonomy and hegemony are seldom questioned. Such epistemological bias wipes out of existence the whole realm of what Michel de Certeau called "the practice of everyday life,"[3] dragging in its wake the understanding of popular culture and, however contradictorily, since it was adopted as an academic fad, of its most ardent redeemer, postmodernism.[4]

Feminists in particular have been quick to point out the reasons behind this common segregation. Theorists like Tania Modleski and Angela McRobbie stress popular culture's subversive potential, indicating how threatening it can ultimately prove to discourses that rely (at times by means of analytical study) on the promotion of class, gender, or race privilege to maintain their stronghold.[5] After all, popular culture, postmodernism, and cultural studies advocate each in its own conflictive way for the emergence of experiences that have been for too long relegated to an intellectual backyard. Furthermore, until very recently the prevailing notion of cultural imperialism assumed a passive spectatorship, ignoring all kinds of creative reception and paradoxically encouraging all sorts of suspicious paternalisms.

It is precisely to such an unacknowledged dynamic reception that Modleski turns in her analyses of genre films, for example, in her discussion of their liberating and pleasurable effects in Manuel Puig's novel-turned-film, *The Kiss of the Spider Woman.* Similarly, McRobbie affirms the importance of appropriation, (mis)quotation, and recycling for black urban music, and Donna Haraway underlines the implicit breaking down of hierarchy in technological interface, tracing it in popular science fiction literature.[6] In Latin America, where a jaded notion of cultural imperialism still helps to maintain the official fictions of national identity, theorists like Néstor García-Canclini are describing the multiple spectator strategies used to meaningfully integrate otherwise arid and abstract discourses. García-Canclini's study of museum goers' sentimental enjoyment of high art, for instance, discovers an unwillingly insubordinate public reaction under an apparently reverential behavior.[7]

What is so threatening about popular culture is not, as has been often affirmed, its supposed mechanical or passive traits, but rather, as Modleski suggests, the enjoyment with which it is integrated into daily practice. The ready pleasure of "trash" magazines and Hollywood films clashes head-on with the aesthetic pleasure worshiped by high-art followers—classicists and modernists alike. Obviously, this aesthetic pleasure is founded on a sophisticated sense of taste whose exquisite sensibility is granted and guaranteed by an education that in turn is made possible by money. Never mind that Benjamin exposed the demise of uniqueness and originality half a century ago in his famous essay on art in the age of mechanical reproduction.[8] No matter how anachronistic, these Romantic notions are still revered today, as is that other stubborn myth, male genius—which goes to show how postmodernism's flattening of history in one eternal present that contains all pasts and futures is indeed an accurate rendition of historical linearity as yet another ideological construct.

Kitsch is, as I contend in chapter 3, one of the best examples of how such aesthetic and intellectual segregations work and of how they paradoxically contain the seeds of their own destruction. For kitsch, generally understood as bad taste or a poor imitation of art and therefore always banished to the margins of artistic practice, does exactly what that practice fears so much: it gathers its motifs randomly and eclectically, fragmenting the cohesion and continuity so cherished by high art, and then dares to re-present them in the most blunt, figurative, and sentimental ways, much to the delight of its "uneducated" consumers and the distress of critics. Kitsch and postmodernism's sharing of an irreverent recycling, a taste for iconography and the artificial, a pleasure in color, gloss, melodrama, and overdetermination, lead me to believe that either postmodernism is kitsch, kitsch is postmodern *avant la lettre,* or both.

While some feminists have been eager to defend the subversive features of postmodernism, claiming that its lack of respect for all kinds of boundaries—that is, historical in the disruption of continuous time, geographical in the enormous exchange between countries and the constant shifting of political and ethnic frontiers, physical in the confusion between the body and electronic apparatuses—opens up new grounds for cultural negotiation, it is precisely the extent of this negotiation that has become the touchstone of postmodernity's legitimacy. Much of the postmodern debate revolves around how social power is articulated and distributed in postmodernism, whose mere existence then becomes contingent on whether it can be qualified as emancipatory or alienating.

This debate became most apparent in the early 1980s, when two European philosophers closed ranks: in one corner, Jean-François Lyotard defended postmodernism's disruption of systemic order as an anarchic force; in the opposite corner, Jürgen Habermas claimed that such disruption only conceals or encourages totalitarian forms of control.[9] Such a discussion attributes to postmodernism an intrinsic function that is, at the very least, controversial, given that postmodernism is a state of things, not a structured and coherent ideology. Postmodernism is then conflated with those discourses that attempt to derive a meaning from it, being perceived alternately as revolutionary, fascistic, hedonistic, or redemptive. Simply put, postmodernism, as popular culture before it, becomes what each interpretation needs it to be, with the theory comfortably sitting in for its object of inquiry.[10] The relativity of such dogmatic positions is apparent in a similar discussion on technology, which Haraway lucidly turns around by proposing how technology can provide destabilizing strategies. In so doing, she shatters the sterile duality that doomed technology to either unquestionable progress or unavoidable social control.

Habermas contributed to this great postmodern divide in more ways than one, refusing to accept postmodernism as substantially different from modernism.[11] Habermas's belief in the healing powers of what he considers the unrealized enlightenment project of modernity denies postmodernism its basic take on that project—that it failed to deliver. And while many of postmodernism's most salient features (disillusionment in what have been called the master narratives of modernity, an unashamed nostalgia for other times, a melancholic overtone) derive from this implicit cultural acknowledgment, others (i.e., the aforementioned eclecticism and breaking down of boundaries) do not hinge at all on modernism, but rather on the plurality and difference it so adamantly tried to purify.

This preoccupation with the origins (in the end, a question of paternity) only succeeds in further confusing the issue of where to go from here. In this respect, I find Marshall McLuhan's lack of demagoguery refreshing. From the 1960s on, McLuhan concentrated on describing the ways in which technology and mass media were transforming culture and speculating, quite accurately as it turns out, on the state of things to come. McLuhan not only refused to be programmatic, he also declined the historiographical genre, favoring instead an image-ridden and fragmentary language that is closer to the phenomena he talks about. He became at once an academic pariah and a best-selling author.[12]

In other words, the postmodern debate has not transcended what Umberto Eco dubbed a couple of decades ago "apocalittici e integrati," referring to the raging polemic about mass media's goods and evils.[13] In the United States this has taken on several nuances of its own, in particular a very postmodern schizophrenia whereby theorists simultaneously love and hate postmodernism. Perhaps its most interesting representative is that peculiar cosmic prophet Jean Baudrillard, the mere mention of whose name produces among debaters an effect similar to that of Moses on the Red Sea. Personally, I confess to an ambiguous relationship, since despite being influenced by Baudrillard's gaze and believing that simulation is fundamental to the understanding of postmodernism, I disagree completely with his final analysis on the disappearance of the referent.[14]

To me, as to several of the theorists mentioned earlier (Deleuze, Haraway), the postmodern flattening of meaning does not imply its disappearance but rather a shifting of registers that allows the formation of new ways of signifying. The flattening of meaning is the exhaustion of certain features that were believed to be intrinsic to it—depth (moving along vertical paradigms that grant a hierarchical position as opposed to moving along a more integrative horizontality), linear causality, univocality—but which turned out to be dispensable when put to the test of new formations or new modes of analyses. This can be clearly appreciated in the extremely hybrid character of contemporary cultural identities, which cannot be defined according to national origin or other types of inherent belonging, but rather by the intricate and extensive web of relationships that different individuals and groups establish in their daily practice and in their imaginary enactments. Or, as Chantal Mouffe says, referring to the postmodern political subject in her inspiring essay on radical democracy, "a subject constructed at the point of intersection of a multiplicity of subject-positions."[15]

So, when Stuart Hall states that "the world dreams itself to be American,"[16] he is referring to the idiosyncratic vision that each culture has of what "being American" is, as well as to the multifarious ways in which American imagery is appropriated and, more often than not, subverted by the mere fact of becoming an icon. A typical example of this process happened recently in Caracas, where the telecommunications system's acute malfunctioning was popularly confronted by the fad of carrying cellular phone look-alike handbags. Such a parody of the uneven fate of transferred high tech in the Third World is underscored by Venezuelans' intact belief in the United States as still representing the most sophisticated technological life-style available. This kind of recycling is far from the contestatory silence Baudrillard attributes to majorities: as opposed to a mute or passive resistance, the ability of collectivities to flex cultural material can be quite eloquent, as long as one is willing to pay attention to these articulations instead of lamenting the waning of conventional discursive arrangements and the loss of a stable referent.

Another figure relevant to the postmodern debate in the United States is Fredric Jameson, mainly because of his pivotal essay on postmodernism as the cultural counterpart of late capitalism, the phase corresponding to high technology and multinational capital.[17] One of the most troubling premises of this proposal is the degree of causality attributed to capitalism in the formation and transformation of culture.

As Modleski, among others, points out, subordinating postmodernism to capitalism reduces the complexities of cultural processes and ignores other important forces at play in their production. Among these, the relevance of flexible and adaptational strategies by collectivities that are either marginalized from or struggling within mainstream hegemony is considerable. The current redefinition of the political sphere by nonpartisan groups and the growing importance and influence of hybrid or deterritorialized cultural identities are among the most radical illustrations of this kind of negotiation, as I argue in chapter 5. Hence the importance of acknowledging that difference has been fundamental to the constitution and life of postmodernism so far.[18]

There can be no doubt, however, about postmodernism's intrinsic relation to capitalism, since the contemporary flattening of meaning has its most explicit antecedent in the shift from use to exchange value. In this sense, one could say that postmodernism is capitalism's currency, more than its cultural logic. Yet to consider that exchange value terminally cancels use value reinforces the tenet of a mechanical and passive reception. Instead, conceiving how consumption allows reinfusing semiotic value onto the commodity (activating it as a sign susceptible to multiple uses) does not deny the dramatic effects of commodity fetishism (i.e., the fragmentation and alienation of subjectivity), but acknowledges how a dynamic, creative consumption is made possible at many levels.

Paradoxically, it might be precisely capitalism's emptying of a univocal and monological use value that enabled the eventual breaking down of conventional ways of meaning formation.[19] By neutralizing the established relationship between an object and its means of production (or, semiotically, between the signifier and the signified) and redefining production in the flat language of market exchange, capitalism deflated uniqueness in favor of its own conventions. In so doing, it unwittingly destabilized a process (on which it nevertheless continued to rely) that grants legitimacy on the grounds of endemic belonging (birth) and seniority (tradition), and in terms of property rights. Thus, the waning of use value can still be lamented as the loss of the "natural," "organic," "unmediated" way of relating to things and experience, the apparent diversity and specificity of original use lost to the homogenizing (however undemocratic) language of exchange value.

Such a fall from grace is almost one with the loss of the aura of originality in the face of mechanical reproduction—a process lucidly analyzed by Benjamin and that, once again, remits us to the paradigms of the popular culture polemic, that is, to a hierarchy of goodness with exclusivity at the top. For the purposes of this prologue, however, what matters is that the process of exchange in itself had until recently a very limited appeal in daily life, where it always appeared under the pragmatic guise of enabling consumption of and access to necessary or fetishized experiences. So, although it suspended use value as a form of immanent meaning, capital did not sit in its place as a stable referent (except in the case of financial speculation in real estate, bonds, art collections, etc.) but rather reached out to an affective investment outside itself.

Postmodernism terminates this arrangement by taking commodity fetishism to the extreme and declaring it the explicit object of its discursive practice rather than hiding it behind a coherent system of meaning. Avoiding a rationale for consumption based on functionality (that is, on possible use), postmodernism sponsors consumption as an autonomous practice. The act of consuming is reedemed as an open-ended possibility of satisfaction, and the interchangeability of commodities is increased to the maximum, as their value is established by circulatory speed and pervasiveness. Constant and unmediated consumption, then, displaces purpose to the point that commodity fetishism becomes an icon, continually replaying its own fragmentation, alienation, and deterritorialization. As a result, postmodernism successfully empties all present and former referential meanings (those that allude to a permanent and unequivocal signification), fracturing the coherence of the discourses that contained them (history, religion, science, etc.). Attempting to reconstitute those meanings at this point is an exercise in nostalgia. The challenge lies in how to take advantage of this suspension of disbelief in order to elicit an entirely different set of meaningful formations. The purpose of this book is to describe how such an apparently finite project as postmodernism, understood as the glorification of consumption, does in fact enable the articulation of novel and often contradictory experiences.

The breaking down of traditional referentiality is manifested in what have become the postmodern trademarks, namely quotation, recycling, pastiche, and simulation. These are indicative not only of the loss of conventional boundaries between production and consumption, but also of an unprecedented mediation in our mode of consuming, which converts all elements of experience into mobile texts that can be transformed at random. Such a distanced reception, indifferent to notions of belonging or loyalty to origins (that is, no longer bound by use value), is best described as a vicarious sensibility (understanding by sensibility a collective disposition toward certain cultural practices): one where experience is lived indirectly, through the intercession of a third party, so to speak, that acts as both its catalyst and its buffer.

Given that all experience is subject to the mediation of a "trained" way of perceiving things (through the structuring power of language in interaction with diverse social ideologies),[20] what I mean here by vicariousness is the indirect impression of those personal events that are usually thought to be lived directly—physical sensation, for example. In contemporary urban experience, feelings, emotions, and sensations are more effectively called upon by media imagery or high-tech simulacra than through direct exposure, a condition Jameson described as the "waning of affect."[21] This is where the impact of late capitalism may be measured, for it is through the agency of high technology that the forsaken relationship between subject and object knows its most radical split, that is, where vicariousness can best be appreciated. In sum, if modern vicarious experience can be conventionally traced back to the kind of confusion Madame Bovary and Don Quijote developed between themselves and the characters of the literature they so loved to read, then postmodern vicarious experience must be acknowledged as a permanent state of existential displacement supported by a technology that has become second nature to us.

Concretely, high technology has induced a confusion between spatial and temporal boundaries, collapsing the conventions that formerly distinguished fantasy from reality and creating a third, quite polemical, cognitive space: that of simulation. As I argue in chapter 1, contemporary culture is caught between the referential and simulative modes of experience. In the former, meaning is produced by indexicality, where signs derive signification from a system of implicit categories and hierarchies that in turn rely on tradition to exercise either affirmative or subversive functions. In simulation, perception is formulated through media (mainly visual images) that discard all types of categorical distinctions—temporal, geographical, and even physical (in the conflation of the organic with the technological)—leaving signs to look at each other intertextually for signification. Simulation enables us to understand, for instance, how contemporary collective memory is made up of television programs instead of a shared notion of history.

The downfall of established referentiality, which can be traced back to the process of commodity fetishism and most recently to recycling strategies for cultural survival, is furthered by the simultaneous disillusionment in modernity's dream of progress. Despite its reversals by the two world wars and the countereffects of industrialism, this dream managed to survive until the 1950s, when it irredeemably began to fade. The failure of modernism's utopic aspirations dislocated the human-centered Romantic belief on which the twentieth century started, leaving in its place a skepticism that can barely muster notions of direction or identity. Without a future to look forward to and with a past whose beliefs modernism itself discredited as stale and insufficient, what remained after the 1950s was a present loaded with a sense of temporal emptiness.

The fragmentation, intertextuality, and massive commodification of everyday life that began with modernity once had a function that has now been totally lost. Modernization strove to create a better world, but belief in a better world is now exhausted, and only its formal mechanisms remain. In the same way that the ruins of the world's fairs, which once grandiosely represented this belief, have aged, so too has modernism, leaving only the dusty shells of its dreams behind. In the midst of this obsolescence, however, new ways of life emerge, more skeptical of those visions that represent the world as moving in only one direction. I believe this moment of new life emerging from the ruins of decaying dreams has been properly called postmodernism.

Highly reminiscent of the continuous metamorphosis of life and death, the paradoxical postmodern condition will be discussed here in the following urban tendencies: the referential emptiness left by high technology and its replenishment with iconographies that belong to other times and other peoples (chapter 3, on kitsch); the replacement of time by a space saturated with temporal allusions (chapter 2, on the retro fashion); the conversion of a postindustrial melancholia fascinated with decay into an iconography that parodies, and often transforms into a political tool, that melancholy (chapter 4, on organic and technological ruins, and chapter 5, on Latin American postindustrial pop).

It is perhaps to the disconcerting quality of postmodernism's continuous transformation of time into space, emptiness into saturation, body into electronics, and absence into presence that one can attribute the premature claim of postmodernism's demise and explain why, like the phoenix, it always emerges stronger from the ashes of such fatuous fires. It is certainly because of that metamorphic quality that I rely in this book on the narrative figure of allegory to describe certain trends in postmodern sensibility. For allegory, as proposed by Benjamin, repre-

Chiyoko and Kay head toward Lady Miyako's temple amid the ruins of Neo-Tokyo. Katsuhiro Otomo, from *Akira*, No. 18. Copyright *Mash • Room* Co., Ltd.; Kodansha, Ltd., Tokyo, 1990.

sents a continuous movement toward an unattainable origin, a movement marked by the awareness of a loss that it attempts to compensate with a baroque saturation and the obsessive reiteration of fragmented memories.[22] Like the myriad experiences of a long journey to a mythic homeland that, in comparison, will prove barren and empty, *Megalopolis* stands and was written for those cities whose greatness emerges from the interstices of their own ruins.

One

Reach Out and Touch Someone

*The dream of technology is to reconstruct human
beings from images.*
Paul Virilio, 1980

High technology has reformulated contemporary perception, in particular the distinction between temporal and spatial paradigms. The increasing importance of visual images in the constitution of a new, simulated space will be compared in this chapter to the psychological
phenomenon of psychasthenia, in which being and surroundings fuse
into one. Similarly, the replacement of a temporal continuum with an
obsessive, paralyzing repetition will be associated with obsessive
compulsive disease, considered by many "the disease of the 1980s."
Along with these perceptual changes, technology is gradually displacing the organic in favor of the cybernetic and the symbolic with the
imaginary, producing a fragmentation of the self that is compensated in
the intensification of pornographic and painful pleasures. Whether
these processes help articulate a totalitarian politics of surveillance
and control or its opposite, a subversive dynamic that trespasses
boundaries and hierarchies, remains the foremost problem in the postmodern debate.

Psychasthenia and the Loss of Spatial Boundaries

Defined as a disturbance in the relation between self and surrounding
territory, psychasthenia is a state in which the space defined by the coordinates of the organism's own body is confused with represented

1

space.[1] Incapable of demarcating the limits of its own body, lost in the immense area that circumscribes it, the psychasthenic organism proceeds to abandon its own identity to embrace the space beyond. It does so by camouflaging itself into the milieu. This simulation effects a double usurpation: while the organism successfully reproduces those elements it could not otherwise apprehend, in the process it is swallowed by them, vanishing as a differentiated entity.

Psychasthenia helps describe contemporary experience and account for its uneasiness. Urban culture resembles this mimetic condition when it enables a ubiquitous feeling of being in all places while not really being anywhere. Architectural transparency, for example, transforms shopping malls into a continuous window display where the homogeneity of store windows, stairs, elevators, and water fountains causes a perceptual loss, and shoppers are left wandering around in a maze. This induced disorientation is heightened by the few, cryptic signs to be found, and it begins in the interminable, spiral search for a parking space (a place in which to place the self). Dislocated by this ongoing trompe l'oeil, the body seeks concreteness in the consumption of food and goods, saturating its senses to the maximum.

Casting a hologramlike aesthetic, contemporary architecture displays an urban continuum where buildings are seen to disappear behind reflections of the sky or merge into one another, as in the downtown areas of most cosmopolitan cities and in the trademark midtown landscape of New York City. Any sense of freedom gained by the absence of clearly marked boundaries, however, is soon lost to the reproduction ad infinitum of space—a hall of mirrors in which passersby are dizzied into total oblivion. Instead of establishing coordinates from a fixed reference point, contemporary architecture fills the referential crash with repetition, substituting for location an obsessive duplication of the same scenario.

Distorted by the artificial neutralization of hourly changes in light, detached from any bodily anchorage, and attacked by repetition, our sense of time becomes so skewed in this aesthetics of transparency and multiplication that it feels as if time had shrunk. Like coming out of a matinee in winter to find the day almost over, there is a feeling of having been robbed of time. Yet these hours are filled with nonstop looking, and the uncanny exhaustion that follows is the result of a sensory overload. Spatial and temporal coordinates end up collapsing: space is no longer defined by depth and volume, but rather by a cinematic

A simulated landscape. From *The Expedition Series*, 1981. Copyright Ruth Thorne-Thomsen and Fotofolio, 1986.

(temporal) repetition, while the sequence of time is frozen in an instant of (spatial) immobility.[2]

A delirious spinning that creates both a spatial mirage and the illusion of passing time may be compared to the rite of passage between childhood and adolescence addressed by many children's stories. Among the most explicit is *Alice's Adventures in Wonderland,* whose main character is suspended in time so that she can freely explore space—the limits of her body—until she is ready to grow up. In the narrative guise of a dream, Alice goes through a series of adventures that confuse her sense of physical identity, in an experience similar to that of postmodern culture: she floats among domestic objects that fail to give her any hold—gravity, like referentiality, has been suspended—and is later completely lost in Wonderland, where signs are deceiving, animals and plants talk and transmute themselves (the Cheshire cat appears metonymically as a smile or stripes), and she grows or shrinks at the arbitrary will of mysterious mushrooms,cakes, and potions.

Complete with a compulsive repetition of time (the Mad Hatter's tea party that starts every other minute) and a voluntary simulation devised to please the fooled senses (the Queen's white roses painted red),

Wonderland is a place where reality and appearance merge into one. In Wonderland logic, time and space are highly evanescent and can only be reconstituted through repetitive linguistic riddles. Yet Alice manages to break with the compulsion that binds the other characters to perpetual loss in a word- and image-filled magic land. She does so by verbally distinguishing between reality and simulation: she questions the logic behind all the characters' games and exposes their "silliness," she names her loss in this strange universe, and she finally dares to call out the Queen of Hearts's theatrics for all they're worth. This open confrontation of authority results in her being chased out of Wonderland's dream.[3]

Alice's recourse to language as a vehicle to establish distinctions — declaring boundaries to avoid psychasthenia and therefore complete her identity formation — isn't as good a possibility for contemporary culture, where verbal language is being gradually displaced by the visual. Nowadays, experience travels in the image circuit; the language of images constitutes a perceptive and expressive currency as well as a collective memory. Images are central to the shaping of identity: largely constituted by the perception of the self as a separate totality, identity must resort to an image to acquire a sense of wholeness. Without such a reflection of the self onto a literal or figurative mirror, self-perception remains fragmented — exactly as if we had never seen our own images in full.[4]

Yet in the midst of technological imagery, establishing one's image has become a difficult task. Like guards seated in front of myriad monitors, urban dwellers participate and assist daily in a new ritual of technological voyeurism that pervades either in fact or potentially the majority of their activities. While most entertainment is based on watching endless films and television programs or playing video games, surveillance cameras register people entering buildings, riding on elevators, carrying out their shopping and banking. Gradually, technological images have become the mirrors in which to look for an identity. Characterized by proliferation and consumptiveness, these ready-made images are easily interchangeable. Like all commodities, they are discardable identities. Mobile and perishable, their traits wane after a few uses.[5]

If verbal language used to provide an entrance to the symbolic (where the social is psychically formulated) while images belonged to an imaginary level, the current prevalence of images means that urban culture is now caught up in an imaginary level. Besides obstructing access to abstraction and undermining the ability of cultural subjects to relate to social institutions, this dramatic displacement of the symbolic implies a restructuring that could possibly subvert the authority on which the symbolic rests and that it, in turn, reproduces. A substantial part of the current debate about contemporary culture's postmodern condition—whether it qualifies as anarchist or as totalitarian—revolves around this rearticulation of the verbal by the visual, implicating a possible reconstitution of language and, by extension, of the hierarchy of power that it entails.[6]

The likelihood of such a subversion stemming from what was at first seen as a threat—the shattering of perceptual referentiality by high technology—will remain a constant argument throughout my discussion of contemporary urban culture. To return to the figure of psychasthenia, it may be held that rather than an organism's inability to distinguish itself from its surroundings, this state can be read as the organism's skillfulness in fusing with those surroundings. Defined thus, psychasthenia would replace rigid hierarchies with easy transitions, representing an altogether new cultural condition.

Obsessive Compulsive Repetition: Simulation and Pornography

Reorganizing space into flatness (lack of depth and volume) and mobility (lack of a fixed axis), monitors and screens have become the new windows of the world, condensing an otherwise vast landscape onto a small frame. This attempt to nail down an elusive reality to its minimalized images is a process that promptly reverses into an organization of reality in which reality becomes contingent on its own representation.[7] In itself, this process is nothing new, but what is particular about how it happens in postmodern culture is the relentless claim to a reality so evasive that it must be erased and renamed simultaneously time after time. In an unprecedented schizophrenia, urbanites are flooded with ads that carry reduction all the way to referential absence, replacing their referents with a reflection or silhouette: a British Airways plane exists only as reflected on a skyscraper, a Kent cigarettes dog is invisible but for the delineation of its silhouette. Simultaneously, perception is bombarded with a reality-intensive campaign obsessed with "the real thing": "You're Living in Real Time—Seiko Time"; "Miller Genuine Draft—As Real as It Gets."

The principles of representation, which worked as long as a certain notion of reality could guarantee their secondary status—the real as a model for representation—have been overturned by a multiplication of images that has literally left no space for such distinctions. This condition is intensified by the increasing permeation of video in the practices of everyday life, as in the computerization of games and services, the emergence of home video, and the expansion of a politics of camera surveillance. Whereas the referential loss triggered by contemporary architecture is related to the perception of space and time in the urban landscape (which transcends the body in scope and dimension), the referential loss induced by video is scaled to human proportion: video interacts actively with people, referring to time and space in direct relation to their bodies.

In fact, both the ownership and the boundaries of the body are at stake in video and in the process it has successfully engaged: simulation. Simulation will be understood here as the establishment of a situation through intertextuality instead of indexicality. In other words, rather than pointing to first-degree references (objects, events) simulation looks at representations of them (images, texts) for verisimilitude. For the purposes of this book, conventional reference and simulacra are equally real, since they are so perceived in contemporary culture.[8]

Although simulation capitalizes on the confusion between itself and conventional reality to gain control over popular perception, it is also empowered by the pleasure mechanisms triggered by its pornographic qualities. In pornography, the boundaries between what is being watched and who is watching barely exist: performance and spectator fuse into one. In a twist of ironic perversion, the anonymity that is necessary for the total release of the imaginary also effaces the viewer's identity. Thus, the pornographic spectator is subjected to a reification similar to that of the pornographic object: both cease to be individuals in order to perform as the figures of a libidinal mechanism. Technological voyeurism leads to a similar suspension of the self, realized in its case for the sake of imagery. Fulfilled by a compulsive repetition that ultimately saturates the libidinal need, pleasure is attained precisely where conventional reality and simulacra (reality and fantasy in pornography) become indistinguishable. As in pornography, the fragmented technological identity fixates on the body as a metaphor for the reproduction of its tortured and unconscious schism.

Contingent on vision and the temporary suspension of the self's boundaries, pornography and simulation depend to a great extent on this compulsive repetition of images to satisfy a perceived lack or absence. Psychologically considered an obsession, compulsive repetition usually implies a lack of resolution between self and space that produces an overlapping of the self onto space. Like psychasthenia, obsessive compulsion disease (OCD) is a "doubting disease," although it resolves its spatial uncertainties in a different manner. A nervous disorder, obsessive compulsion is a disconnection between body and mind, a situation of mutual distrust where all acts are suspect and self-perception is unreliable. This uncertainty provokes an extreme worry that acts itself out in the form of rituals. Lasting for hours, these rituals consist in the painful replay of an image, association, or feeling: washing one's hands forty times a day, being unable to leave for work for fear that the windows are not well shut, driving miles back to make sure that no one was hit on the way. Obsessive compulsion paralyzes people to the point where most of their time is spent mechanically repeating their fixation—in other words, trying to exorcise the emptiness left by doubt with the multiplication of its figures. More common than schizophrenia, agoraphobia, or panic disorder, OCD has been found to affect about 3 percent of the U.S. population, with half the cases starting in childhood.[9]

Whereas psychasthenia merges into space through a deceleration of time so radical that it is considered a step back from life into death, obsessive compulsion, in keeping with technological expedience, resorts to speed as its way of covering the identity vacuum opened by doubt. The obsessive compulsive person gets stuck in time, which repeats itself as a futile gesture of imitation caught in a twilight zone between the organism and its setting. An artificial fulfillment of space, obsessive repetition is at the core of the process of simulation in which postmodern culture is engaged. It is not by chance that just when the body is struggling to survive referential loss, obsessive compulsion disease and its bodily fixation should emerge so dramatically.

In these circumstances, the concurrence of physical pain and mechanical violence acquires inordinate reality attributes, accounting for the ever-growing fascination with death and mutilation images in popular culture and mass media. In his novel *Crash!*, J. G. Ballard systematically re-creates car accidents as the occasions for an otherwise unattainable intensity, one that is largely erotic and that is conjugated on the frenzied formula of sex and death.[10] Repetitive compulsion, voyeurism, and sex without a body: pornography. As the body disappears, it is imaginarily reconstructed from its leftover fragments and traces. The current politics of sexual repression comes from and paves the way back to this absence, disavowing the (punished) body from an enjoyment that is relegated to the realm of the imaginary—the narratives of pornography and perversion.

The pornographic pleasure derived from watching physical pain is illustrated in the increase in murder and gore shown on network television. Technological voyeurism literally climaxed in the summer of 1986 with the coverage of Jennifer Levin's murder in Central Park.[11] Having aroused a lot of interest for its combination of rich white teenagers, "wild" sex, and fatal violence, the "preppie murder" case was transformed into a pornographic spectacle. Initially displaced from murder to female lust—in the speculation about Levin's "sexual" diary entries—the case was eventually diffused by legal technicalities that centered on Levin's body and the extent of the damage it suffered. It was not Levin's murder but her sexuality and her corpse that stimulated public attention and media hype.

In keeping with the erasure of Jennifer Levin behind the marks on her body, her murderer practically disappeared behind his own video image. Both in his contradictory confessional tapes—whose public circulation made them almost a home entertainment—and in the "playful" recreation of his strangling of Levin with a doll for the camera, Chambers became a totally unreal person, the star of a grotesque video charade. It was this last tape that inspired Fox's television reenactment of Levin's death in a program that attained such an immense rating success that three years later it was being made into a television film.[12]

True to the seduction strategy of promising and not delivering, rather than showing the doll tape in its entirety as it had announced, Fox used it as a bait for a two-hour program of its own making. Mixing the most striking piece of the tape, where Chambers is laughingly strangling the doll for the camera—in a quite literal illustration of the way his crime was handled publicly—Fox's program extensively recreated the two young people's relationship, their backgrounds, and the night of the crime. Using footage of their homes and their parents, childhood photographs, and clips of Chambers's videos, the story was fully detailed. The remaining gaps—what happened the night of the crime—were covered with the station's own script: two actors, their faces slightly shadowed so that their impersonation remained ambiguous, played out the different scenes of the meeting, the walk to the park, and the murder. Even if the struggle that took place between the two was conspicuously missing—a struggle that has been extensively documented in court and that makes the program's supposed objectivity even more

As the body disappears, it is imaginarily reconstructed from its leftover fragments and traces. Ads from the *Village Voice*, January 15, 1991.

suspicious—the fact remains that viewers got to participate quite fully in one of the most famous sexual stories of the year.

As in the infamous "snuff" films, where the women performing sado-masochistic scenes were actually killed on camera to enhance the pornographic intensity of the videos, Jennifer Levin's murder was made into an entertainment of the most perverse degree.[13] Her death became a simulation of itself, its connection to the event contingent only on the reproduction of its images: pictures, video clips, and so on. Instead of helping establish what did happen that night, the exhaustive visual documentation generated by this case made it hyperreal, only succeeding in blurring it further. Not only did fictive reenactments such as the one produced by Fox mask the actuality of the crime, even the lengthy forensic inquiries as to exactly how many seconds it took to kill her (based on the marks left on her neck) replaced the fact that she had been murdered at all. In a way, Levin was murdered twice: first at the hands of Chambers, and then in the Fox studios.[14]

Unwittingly, Jennifer Levin was used for the full-fledged release of a fairly recent and polemical television genre known as docudrama, a fictitious account of events whose claim to objectivity is based on its arbitrary donning of the documentary etiquette. Docudrama is a good example of the co-option of leftist and independent language by a conservative discourse. Since the documentary genre has been widely used to discredit mainstream stories, broadcast television has struck back with a vengeance by usurping the genre, stripping it of its main attribute (a nonfictional relation of events) and transforming it into the most threatening of all possible accounts: that which refuses to accept its own subjectivity. The perfect simulacrum, docudrama is a fearless mixture of facts and fiction that professes authority on the grounds of image legitimacy.[15]

The Organic/Technological Interface

If the fragmentation of contemporary identity is reproduced in referential absence and the pleasures of pain are induced by a pornographic technology, it should come as no surprise that the body has been rendered totally vulnerable. In the same contradictory manner that advertising promotes the reality/unreality of a referent, bodies have become the locus of a fierce battle between permanence and evanescence. Thus, at the same moment that a culture of youth and fitness obsesses over exercising and dieting, the AIDS epidemic strikes tens of thousands, disabling one of the body's principal protection mechanisms.[16] The last bastion of a precarious sense of identity, the body has turned into the ruin of its own image: against senility, disability, and physical decay, mass culture projects images of immaculate health and happiness, and ultimately the cybernetic, or half-technological, body.

The protection of the body as a last refuge for identity assumes that humanness is a natural attribute, locating it in the realm of the organic as opposed to the artificial, however fictive such organicity might be. As a distinctive and privileged characteristic, humanity is bound to win against alien creatures and gigantic animals, whose attributed lack of or inferior spirituality can only enhance the uniqueness of being human. Yet this superiority begins to falter with artificial beings, whose mechanical or technological bodies were not supposed to house a "heart." From their very inception in Mary Shelley's *Frankenstein*— whose subtitle is significantly *The Modern Prometheus*[17]—artificial beings' emotional faculties have been a cultural problem. While for a few decades this was resolved in the simple dualism between organic body and robot, the technological advances that made their fusion possible in the first place finally rendered this duality untenable, as *Blade Runner* (Ridley Scott, 1982) clearly illustrates.[18]

Having turned into a cult classic because of its complex treatment of a high-tech reality, *Blade Runner* explores the threat posed to the body by technological reproduction and questions the assumptions underlying this menace. As in legendary Atlantis, the underwater city whose perfection led to self-destruction, human beings in *Blade Runner* have technologically replicated themselves to such an exact degree that their own existence is now endangered. Created as slaves, replicants develop in time the only feature that distinguished them from their makers: emotions. Like all simulacra, replicants undermine the notion of an original by disavowing any differences between themselves and their creators.[19]

Blade Runner narrates the ensuing life and death struggle between humans and replicants. Beyond immediate survival, this fight is about validating the robotic experience—that is, admitting that neither is humaneness exclusively organic nor is the organic a guarantee of humanity. The angry extermination of replicants by the same world that produced them provides clear proof of the lack of empathy and affection that "real" people are capable of. Human beings in this film are in a state of spiritual decay metaphorically portrayed in the condition they've brought upon Earth, a planet so unhealthy it must be aban-

doned for better (however artificial) colonies. Although the precariousness of human feeling is conveyed in the film by the main character's
ambivalent attitude toward the replicants he must kill, it is in the novel
on which *Blade Runner* is based that such lack of feeling can be appreciated to its full extent. In *Do Androids Dream of Electric Sheep* by
Philip K. Dick, humans are so out of touch with their own emotions that
they must resort to machines in order to feel anything at all.[20]

In transforming experience into the common language of information, modern technology has achieved a maximum quantitative efficiency at the cost of heterogeneity.[21] No longer distinguishable from
computers, the body is thought of as a system whose parts are per-
fectible and replaceable. Slowly, body and computer have begun to
exchange their peculiar traits: the body becomes mechanized at the
same rate that technology is made human. This process can be observed in the advertising campaigns of AT&T, one of the largest multinational telecommunication conglomerates. Extremely concerned with
marketing its products and services in a "consumer-friendly" way,
AT&T assures its customers that its huge technological deployment is
harmless and unthreatening. To this end, it equates technology and
people. In its "Reach Out and Touch Someone" campaign, for instance, sophisticated telephone communications were attributed a
human tactile quality: by calling someone you love (no other calls were
contemplated in this campaign) you could actually touch that person.
Consistent with this approach, AT&T devised a public information
center, "INFOQuest," a sort of information playland in New York City
where people can experiment with the basics of that technological empire for free. In an ultra high tech ambience of transparencies,
chromes, and monitors, the main AT&T products—light-wave communications, computer software, and microchips—are displayed and explained, while the accompanying narrative emphasizes their personal
qualities and stresses the American stronghold of individuality and
freedom: consumer choice.

From here to a cyborg reality there is one step, and it has already
been made by science fiction. In the blockbuster *RoboCop* (Paul
Verhoeven, 1987), a dead cop is reconstructed as a robot whose faint
human memories provide him with feelings of vengeance and
justice—an eerie anticipation of the police state to come. Even comic-
book superheroes—earthlings and aliens—have become a hybrid of
organism and technology: "Circuit Breaker" of the transformer robots
series is a woman who used her electronic genius to convert her de-

stroyed body into a top electronic apparatus. Fiction is not far from fact in the case of transformer robots. In the summer of 1988, CBS broadcast in New York an interview with two "Decepticons," members of a gang of black high-school students who had been violently intimidating communities in Manhattan and Brooklyn. About 450 in number, the Decepticons took their name from the homonymous evil transformer-robots, who are emotionless and invulnerable. As their name implies, Decepticons are deceivers, and their appearance is misleading: they look human, but are really robots. Ironically, the broadcast furthered this confusion between organism and mechanism by digitizing the faces of the interviewees. In scrambling the lines of the video to safeguard the gang members' identities, CBS unwittingly reproduced the effect these kids sought—interface. With the boundary between their organic selves and the technological apparatus that transmitted their images effectively blurred, the Decepticons appeared to viewers to be technological bodies.[22]

Both an organic and a technological body, the fictional cyborg represents the ultimate spatial transgression, an accomplishment that it shares with holograms. Possessing the best of both worlds, cyborgs combine human attributes with the perfection of a technological anatomy, signifying a final breakdown of the boundaries between spirit and matter. Cyborgs are the "natural" extension of the boundary erosion carried out by the domain of technological imagery—the offspring, so to speak, of that peculiar reality that hides the Levin/Chambers case behind a wall of video images and produces Decepticons. A product of cybernetics (the study of communication and control systems such as the brain and the nervous system), cyborgs are the imaginary result of a sophisticated information society where everything is conceived in terms of organization. The need to gather and categorize information involves some of the compulsive controlling procedures found in pornography, namely fragmentation (mutilating information so it fits a code), homogenization (of the information into a predictable code or narrative), repetition (difference is reduced to variations on the same theme), apparent choice, and a voyeuristic control exercised digitally. Information processing is mechanically indistinguishable from the politics of surveillance, which would not be possible without it. Furthermore, information processing lends an objective sheen to what is often a controlling perversion of the voyeuristic type.[23]

Dismembered and stripped of anything personal, the subject of information processing stands alone against the ubiquitous but anony-

Circuit Breaker converted her destroyed body into a top electronic apparatus by wrapping printed circuits around her crippled limbs. From ''More Than Meets the Eye,'' *The Transformers*, vol. 1, no. 45. Copyright Marvel Entertainment Group Inc., 1988.

mous eye of institutionalized agencies of control, either public (governmental interference in people's rights through tax files, drivers' licenses, permits, mail) or private (at work, in stores, in intimate life).[24] The scope of information processing contributes to an atmosphere of total exposure, where everything is under surveillance and nothing can be hidden. In the same way that *Blade Runner*'s main character, Deckard, dissects a photograph with his monitor and uncovers a clue imperceptible to the human eye—a manufactured fish scale in a bathtub—he is susceptible in his own home to the invasion of the Coca-Cola/ Japanese woman blimp that "spies" on him through his window. In *Blade Runner,* traditional surveillance has been surpassed by a mixture of reality and simulacra that attains a sophisticated state of control—one where surveillance devices are no longer necessary, since a prevailing condition of tension and vigilance has successfully permeated everybody's imaginary. In situations like these, the private eye is no longer distinguishable from the suspect.[25]

Information and surveillance systems are made even more dangerous by their fallibility. Accidents like incorrect data entries and malfunctions can alter reality and produce nonexistent identities or switch existing ones, even deleting people from the annals of the living and resurrecting the dead.[26] Their attributed omnipotence and objectivity, however, ensure that their "word" has more authority than a human being's. Technology seems to be doing more than taking over and transforming space: it is creating a continuous state of self-doubt, hesitation, and confusion.

Although the obsession with systems articulates J. G. Ballard's novels, he is quick to distinguish the perverse connections between information and control as a result of technology's interaction with a culture that already contains these distortions, and not as an exclusive product of technology itself. Donna Haraway goes even further, arguing in favor of cyborgs on the grounds that the technological breakdown of physical barriers can have beneficial social uses. Haraway proposes the cyborg as a metaphor for a new, hybrid social body that would enable the empowered integration and free flow of discourses, such as feminism, that have been marginalized for going against traditional standards.[27] Even if high tech has been put to the service of conservative uses— insistence on family values, subordination of women, increased automatization of middle- and low-income workers—Haraway claims that the disruption of hierarchy and traditional boundaries caused by the tech-

PRIME PEOPLE DETECTORS
The automatic Talking Robot sounds off with your recorded voice whenever anyone comes within range of its built-in passive infrared (PIR) detector. Only 6" tall and 3½" wide, the powerful robot continuously monitors an area 30 degrees on either side and 17 feet in front of where it is placed and presents your message to anyone that intrudes on its space!
Although the robot cannot physically attack an intruder, its digital voice synthesizer (yours) is loud and clear as in, "you have 45 seconds to vacate the area," which should give the intruder pause. Not a tape recorder, the Talking Robot is a solid-state digital voice synthesizer. Solid-state semi-conductors insure long-life use. After your message, it recycles automatically. It's ideal at the front door, or to leave messages for the family: Say "Hi, be back in 15 minutes," or any recorded news, warning or safety tip you like up to 16 second recorded news, warning or safety tip you like. Includes AC/DC transformer, power cord and instructions.
Automatic Talking Robot #4125 $125.00 (3.15)

WANT TO HEAR WHAT'S GOING ON IN YOUR HOME OR OFFICE WHILE YOU'RE AWAY?
The Teletaf remote monitoring device lets you listen in through your regular line from any phone in the world—and the telephone dialed will not ring! Place one in the nursery when you run next door, listen for possible intruders, many more uses. Simply snap the Teletaf's modular plug into a modular telephone jack in the area you wish to monitor, switch on the system. The sensitive microphone will pick up a whisper 35 feet away! After 80 second or when you hang up, the Teletaf automatically discontinues monitoring. Want to listen further? Just call back. Switch off upon your return for normal telephone operation. 80-second cycle-on time required. Needs no batteries.
The Teletaf remote monitor #4170 $99.95 (4.50)

FINALLY, AN INTERCOM YOU SIMPLY PLUG IN— NO WIRING, NO INSTALLATION
The new two-way Novi FM wireless intercom is a new way to bring the family together! With everyone doing his or her own thing in the house, the intercom is the perfect communication device. And this is the first intercom that utilizes phase locked loop (PLL) circuitry for clear, hi-fidelity voice transmission that cuts out noise or interference up to a range of 1500 feet. After plugging these units into AC outlets, press Call to page, press Talk to converse, press Lock for lengthy, hands-free conversations, to monitor the baby's nursery or an empty room. Two channels (A,B) let you switch to cut out possible interference. Order extra sets and assign these channels to separate quarters or garage. Great for office or home. High-impact plastic with power/in-use LED indicators, on/off and volume controls. May be wall mounted. Manufacturer's Warranty.*
FM wireless intercom #4405 set $69.95 (4.00)

NEW FREEDOM! WIRELESS HEADSET LETS YOU LISTEN IN PRIVACY FROM ANY ROOM
The Wireless Headset lets you listen to any audio unit in your home! Simply connect the miniature, FCC approved UHF transmitter to the audio output or headphone jack of your TV, VCR, home audio system or CD player amplifier, and voila! Crisp, clear, brilliant sound will be received through the palm-size receiver to the high-fidelity headset with comfortable padded earphones. You can even adjust the volume on the receiver that handily clips on your belt. Make dinner and listen to the TV news in the den; work in the garage while listening to music on your CD player; listen and watch TV in bed without disturbing the sleeper next to you or tangling with a wire connected to the TV!
Wireless Headset #4345 $99.95 (2.60)

Everything is under surveillance, nothing can be hidden. Ad from Life Force Technologies, Ltd., catalog, 1988.

nologization of daily life can potentially enable the emergence of new cultural practices.

This allowance for marginal takeover and redefinition might be illustrated in the impact of "breakdancing" in the last decade. By creating a dance of mechanical movements that resembles video and filmic slow motion—simulating a breakdown of speed and therefore of the il-lusion of continuous movement—black New York teenagers captured the attention of blacks and nonblacks worldwide. However restricted to the spectacular, poor black boys succeeded both in creating a sophis-ticated simulation of technology and in becoming the object of admi-ration and imitation, no small feat for youths who are generally either ignored or looked down upon and usually regarded as unskilled.

The fictional creation of the cyborg has shaken the assumption of an identity contingent on a natural humanity. The fear and resentment of a technological takeover and concomitant displacement of organic hu-maneness contribute to the fierce reaction against laboratory babies, artificial insemination, euthanasia, and even abortion—often carried out by the same people who otherwise happily participate in techno-logical consumption. Such is the contradiction of the Reagan-Bush years and their aftermath: an unprecedented technological escalation accompanied by the insistence on reality and traditional values.[28]

Struggling over the Vanishing Body

Confused by transparent and repetitive spatial boundaries, discon-nected from the body by a video landscape that has stolen its image, haunted by a technology that threatens to take the last bastions of what once seemed inalienably human, contemporary identity bounces be-tween radically opposite possibilities. It can opt for a psychasthenic dissolution into space, merging into the multilayered cityscape like so many other images, floating in the complete freedom of unrootedness; lacking a body, identity then affixes itself to any scenario like a transi-tory and discardable costume. Or it can profit from the crossing of boundaries, turning the psychasthenic process around before its final thrust into emptiness, benefiting from its expanded boundaries. This entails disabling fragmentation and category, which have impeded the peaceful interaction of difference and reduced identity to throbbing fixations—a perverse voyeurism that finds its only intensity in the ulti-mate splitting of desire and the body.

Contemporary schizophrenia confronts heterogeneity with neutral-ization, confusion with repression, and referential absence with an in-formational deadweight, legitimizing surveillance as the only mecha-nism that can provide both control and pleasure to a culture lost in its own specter. Since the struggle is over the body—its fragmentation and disappearance—it is only fitting that the body be the arena in which all stakes are claimed. The control strategies that began to be applied with the excuse of AIDS (compulsory blood and urine tests, institutional segregation) have spread to the more densely inhabited terrain of drug consumption, enabling a state of siege that has violently redefined the limits of the public and the private. The battle over where the body starts and ends has of course extended to the issue of reproduction, substituting the rights of the unborn for those of the born, in the same awkward metonymic exchange that allows the phone sex hype to replace body with voice.

Perhaps the most striking account in the struggle over the vanishing body is its very literal manifestation in the fight over territory. In New York City, the value of people has sunk below that of objects, as the growing numbers of homeless people—bodies without homes, dislocated to leave room for real-estate speculation—bear witness. The substitution of use for exchange value is seldom so blatant: families inhabit parks and streets while hundreds of habitable buildings stand by empty, awaiting the best market opportunity to be reopened. This bodily displacement is even more violent than a war, because homelessness is a condition of slow deterioration and hardly appreciated heroisms. It is as if contemporary culture had developed a psychasthenic myopia by virtue of which people living on the street seem a natural extension of the urban scenario.

Two

Lost in Space

The case of the Phyllia *[leaf insects] is even
sadder: they browse among themselves, taking
each other for real leaves, in such a way that one
might accept the idea of a sort of collective
masochism leading to mutual homophagy, the
simulation of the leaf being a provocation to
cannibalism in this kind of totem feast.*
Roger Caillois, 1938

The postmodern confusion of time and space, in which temporal
continuity collapses into extension and spatial dimension is lost
to duplication, transforms urban culture into a gigantic hologram capable of producing any image within an apparent void. In this process,
time and space are transformed into icons of themselves and consequently rendered into scenarios. Among the most conspicuous of
these mise-en-scènes is the 1950s and 1960s retro fashion. A highly
profitable nostalgic comeback, this cultural trend may be read as a parodic attempt to broach some contemporary fears, most notably the replacement of the organic and human by the technological. The iconography produced in the space age engaged the issues of time and
space allegorically, a metaphorical process that will help elucidate certain mechanisms of mainstream representation and meaning.

The increasingly swift interchangeability of signs promotes a certain
homogenization: lacking the specificity given them by history (time)
and location (space), what once were cultural emblems (icons, dress,
music, language) and functioned as indexes of a peculiar cultural
identity now float freely as commodities, their ethnic quality further so-
liciting market voraciousness and enhancing their value. In this sense,
signs' traits seem to respond more to the logic of exchange than to the
conventions of a cultural identity, further weakening the already precarious dualism between tradition and modernity.[1]

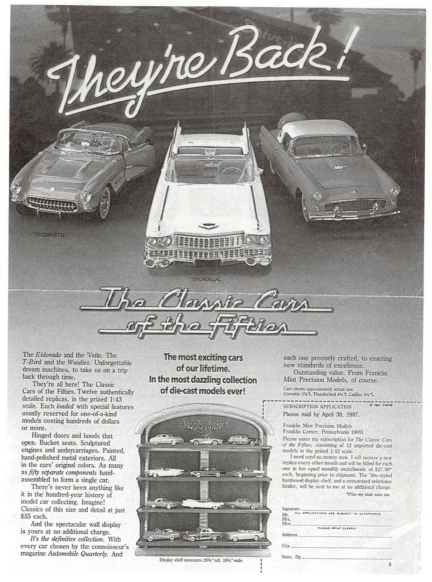

Ad from *Discover*, April, 1987.

An interesting example of such a decontextualization of signs is the Greek-column revival fad that has taken over interior design in the past few years. Reproduced in isolation from the structures they used to adorn (temples, churches, state and corporate buildings), columns now appear fragmented and in ruins, framing in neon light the en-

trances to photocopying shops, ornamenting fried-meat fast-food lun-
cheonettes, and multiplying as lamp supports. Loaded with the heritage of antiquity, columns used to inspire the awe of the "birth of
civilization" days—their grandiosity, permanence, and classic beauty.
Having lost all this traditional authority, columns now stand as orna-
ments whose legacy is valuable only as a stylized intertextuality. As
such, they add the charm of an antiquity familiar to everyone while ignoring all the classic values. Their indexical value as signs of power
and authority has been transformed into an intertextual one. What matters now is the columns' vague allusion to a history that has become a
still scenario where eras, locations, and characters figure merely as
props.[2]

Free from the restraints of a fixed referentiality, signs can travel
openly through the circuits of meaning, ready to be taken up or left arbitrarily, connecting in ways that were previously unthinkable. That
signs no longer convey depth but rather remain at surface value
speaks of their break with the symbolic, where signification is produced by a strategic positioning within an elaborate and hierarchical
system of presence and absence, as in the concrete representation of
abstract meaning. As opposed to such a system, the current constitution of signs occurs through allegorical signification, which highlights
the here and now of the sign, reaffirming its most concrete attributes.[3]

The Allegorical Compensation for Cultural Anxiety

Allegory's metaphorical comment on reality is the perfect emblem for a
perception always one step removed from its source. It is in the distinct
relation of the symbol and the allegory to a source that usually represents some kind of origin or truth that their respective qualities are most
clearly illustrated. For, while the symbol represents a condensation between signifier and signified (and between referent and representation), allegory reenacts the opposite, the impossibility of that condensation ever taking place.

Symbolic condensation displaces signifying distance (difference) in
hierarchical positioning: the symbol and what it stands for are understood as one and the same, yet meaning is more important than representation. Allegory, on the other hand, does not establish this ambiguous equivalence, mainly because it is defined by desire and lack:
allegory seeks the return to that founding, original truth, but does not
achieve it. Allegory, then, becomes the trace of a failed attempt, an in-

complete movement that can only reproduce itself every time it tries to overcome that signifying gap.[4] The inability to accept this limitation determines allegory's melancholic character, and its obsessive attempts render allegorical production baroque and saturated. Yet it is precisely in this failure to achieve condensation that the arbitrariness of the symbolic gesture is exposed. Allegorical distance underlines the constitutive difference between referent and representation. So, while allegory fails to reestablish an origin and its consequent truth, it succeeds in pointing out the obviously constructed quality of symbolic truth.[5]

A narrative figure that constructs meaning horizontally, allegory privileges continuity (or its lack) over vertical selection. It is this syntagmatic extension that determines allegory's paradoxical relation to time. For while structurally allegory overdetermines meaning by reiterating it in different registers, this repetition, like that of obsessive compulsive disease, cancels the progression of time, replacing historical meaning with scenification. Such a transfer of time to space is mainly a result of the exhaustion of cultural assumptions that provided a coherent, comprehensive vision of the world, as represented primarily in the symbolic unity of matter and spirit. This disruption of the symbolic unity radically transforms experience, since it no longer is connected to a transcendent, abstract meaning. Instead, experience becomes intense and material, seeking the confirmation of its existence in the present and concrete. Only the most explicit manifestations satisfy this desire, giving rise to figuration that finds in allegory its perfect expression. Having left the notion of totality behind, allegory replenishes the ensuing vacuum with the multiplication of signifiers.

The iconographic frenzy of the 1950s and 1960s masked a desperate struggle with an old, underlying death that had been sealed with Romanticism: that of spiritual faith. It was an attempt to believe unambivalently and wholeheartedly in the good of industrialization and in material production as a replacement for a lost sense of existential meaning. Similarly, the rediscovery of the tangibility and visuality of signs in the 1980s enabled allegory, a sensory experience particularly relevant and gratifying at a moment when perception is mediated by the same technology that displaced transcendental meaning. In this sense, the referential emptiness often attributed to postmodern culture can be accounted for by a phenomenon whose complexity surpasses a reductive neutralization of signs. This phenomenon may be described as the opening of a perceptual gap that produces a high degree of cultural anxiety and that is the result of a cultural unwillingness or inability to fully accept the world of simulacra. The consequence of the shift from an indexical to an intertextual constitution, this perceptual gap represents an instinctual resistance to the overwhelming and un-bounded fluidity of a world where signs are neither tied to any one dis-course nor broken down into categories and hierarchies.[6]

Since this gap between referential and simulated experience must be filled in order to soothe the anxiety it produces, it is not surprising that a tendency toward saturation should follow—hence an attempt to fill the perceived emptiness quantitatively, making sure that no space is left blank lest the anxiety filter through it. Furthermore, insofar as the loss is one of tangibility (touch has been replaced with images and sounds in high technology), culture turns toward those forms that pro-vide a notion of concreteness as an imaginary compensation, explain-ing allegory's popularity. Consequently, the perceptual gap is covered by an ambivalent process: it is saturated by signs that recall tangibility while simultaneously, by their nature as signs, eluding it. Indicative of this phenomenon is the retro 1950s and 1960s fashion, in which the desire for intensity and the recirculation of a heavily iconographic im-agery unite to resolve the spatial confusion of contemporary identity in its own terms.

Its referent hardly one generation old, space age retro is attracted by an imagery of progress only possible to an apocalyptical fin de siè-cle as a melancholic appropriation—one that refuses to accept death, fetishistically clinging to memories, corpses, and ruins.[7] The space age produced a rich imagery of a now-unthinkable future and believed in it fiercely. The massive recirculation of its cultural artifacts (films, tele-vision sitcoms, songs, clothes, cars) appears as an attempt to either simulate or cannibalize the fervent hope that produced such a tremen-dous number and variety of icons. This vicarious compensation for a perceptual gap may be compared to what Fredric Jameson called the "waning of affect" in contemporary culture: an alienated condition re-quiring a cultural overdose of intense emotions. Cops-and-robbers television serials, catastrophe films, and the growing tendency toward presenting all events as extreme situations, replacing their lack of con-text with a high degree of emotionality, are emblematic of this condi-tion. Paradoxically, this overdose numbs our capacity for emotional em-pathy while attempting to compensate for its disintegration.[8]

Whereas in the space age the fear of technology was related to the threat of nuclear warfare, in the last decades of the twentieth century it is the cybernetic displacement of the organic by the robotic that is perceived as deadly. In both cases the ambivalence toward technology becomes a question of spatial control—determining the boundaries of nation, culture, and body—and is expressed quite consistently as a territorial struggle. This figurative spatialization extends to include even temporality. Projected onto a future perceived as within a generation's grasp—as opposed to a relatively distant and utopic future that would belong to "other people"[9]—time was frozen in a capsule where chronological progression was replaced by locus: the space age. The space fantasy constituted the 1950s and 1960s imagination as illustrated in television serials like "Lost in Space" (1965-68) and "Star Trek" (1966-69), in which spaceships represent a mobile society that travels, immutable, in a timeless but adventure-ridden universe. In these programs, as in most of the science fiction films produced during this period, the prevailing narrative is not one of temporal continuity (appropriate in an epic genre concerned with history: inheritance, aging, youth, etc.) but rather one of spatial frontiers, specifically the issues of expansion and invasion. Consequently, the distinction between outer space, which became the territory of futuristic projections, and the body, a sort of inner space extremely susceptible to harm, enabled the metaphoric manifestation of an identity conflict that implicated the most basic ontological elements. It is this paradigm that contemporary culture takes from the space age, although accommodating the paradigm to its own needs.

The iconography produced in the 1950s and 1960s that began to be recycled in the 1980s is then almost exclusively articulated by spatial metaphors and a spatial narrative that literally "conquer" space—and time—with their allegorical profusion. How this iconography enables an imaginary control will be discussed in the production of a futuristic aesthetics of everyday life; concomitantly, the fears this control is designed to keep at bay will be seen emerging in the apparently innocuous area of mass entertainment, namely the science fiction genre. Finally, the recycling of the space age iconography will be addressed as a self-conscious and artificial appropriation that fulfills a necessary cultural function.[10]

Progressing toward a Future in Ruins

The prolific aesthetics of the late 1950s and early 1960s is imbued with this period's notion of the future. Architecture and design in particular denote this temporal displacement with an aerial, "futuristic," intergalactic aesthetics that is predominantly geometrical and curvilinear and is known as biomorphism. Angles and circles act as metaphors for speed, space, rockets, and planets, while curves convey a fluidity that is not only representative of the absence of gravity but also overflowing with verbal and visual allusions to space. Likewise, stars are a popular motif, maps imply a much-desired universality, and locations are often named after astronomical entities.[11]

Such a dramatic meshing of living and outer space is clearly indicative of the period's unrelenting spatial articulation, which attempted to combine function with aesthetics to produce a meaning replete with temporal connotations: progress. Both the distribution and the conformation of architectural space followed the prevailing dictum of a time when the postwar urban repopulation required housing expansion. Highrises and housing projects were built according to a design that privileged an open visual field over spacious housing conditions, favoring vertical growth and crowding over more humane, horizontally extended urban layouts. The latter, in turn, were characteristic of the emergent European satellite cities, although at the expense of suburban isolation. The emigration of Italian and French architects to Latin America generated some of the most amazing extravaganzas of this spatial aesthetics. In Caracas and São Paulo, for example, architecture shot upward like a rocket, reversing weight distribution (heavy buildings were mounted on curve-shaped pillars, terraces and balconies protruded precariously, and entire houses were hung from cliffs), creating a lightweight feeling, an apparent defiance of the laws of gravity.[12]

Discarding what seemed useless and working toward maximum gain, the logic of efficiency that commanded this architecture trusted that the thrust of a daring design would suffice to substantially alter reality. So did science and technology. Together with an escalating production of commodities and an emphasis on the nuclear family, postwar scientific development sought to achieve absolute control over matter by making of outer space the displaced vehicle through which to imagine material security. It was as if the production of a new scenario would by itself guarantee a different world, marked by automatic efficiency, where people might regain a lost sense of control with the help of mechanical command. Pushing a button, an early form of digitalism, became the effortless key to the dream of progress.

The full range of this dream was ambitiously exhibited in what may be the most representative phenomenon of modernity's industrializa-

The 1950s aerial architecture in Caracas, Venezuela. Photo copyright Carmen Spencer, 1959.

tion and universalistic scope: the world's fairs. Between 1851 and 1970, thirty-four major fairs were staged, reaching a climax in the New York World's Fairs of 1939 and of 1964-65, where the futuristic notion was introduced as a substantial element. A look at the 1964-65 fair will show the extent to which the space age created a perfect world of consumption under the guise of progress, exploiting to the maximum the notion of conquering space.

Although the New York World's Fair of 1964-65 used an earth globe—the Unisphere—as an icon of its internationality, it was laid out with broader cosmogonic perspectives in mind. A map shows two main centers, the Fountain of the Planets and the Unisphere, around which, like moons, most of the exhibit pavilions gravitate. Located at the Pool of Industry, the Fountain of the Planets is faced by the Court of the Universe and surrounded by two concentric rings: the Promenade of Industry and the Avenue of Progress. These in turn lead into the Avenues of Enterprise, Invention, Common Research, and Discovery, embracing such unlikely planets as the General Electric, Continental Insurance, IBM, American Interiors, and Boy Scouts pavilions. Establishing a second galaxy, the Unisphere, at the Court of the Pres-

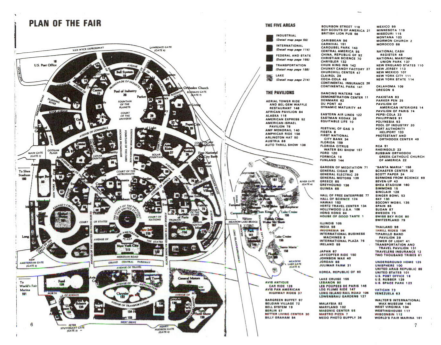

Map of the 1965 World's Fair in New York. From *The Official Guide to the World's Fair*. Copyright the editors of Time Life Books, 1965.

ident of the United States, unites the Courts of the Astronauts, the States, and the Nations and serves as center to the Avenues of the Americas and of Africa. Under the influence of the Lunar and Solar Fountains—which connect to the first galaxy by way of the Courts of the Moon and of the Sun respectively—the Unisphere can be found at the center of the countries' exhibits, where such intriguing pavilions as Tribes, British Lion Pub, and Berlin stand alongside Guinea, Hong Kong, Central America, China, and India, all under the Swiss Sky Ride. Below the Unisphere, the United States, because of either its hosting function or its global outreach, had a whole section for itself; New York City, Hollywood, Alaska, and Westinghouse were among the exhibits.

A microcosm where astronomical and geographical entities mix with each other and with corporations to produce a united vision of the world, the 1964-65 New York World's Fair succeeded in equalizing such disparate elements merely by throwing them onto a common map and subordinating them to exchange value. This equalization is the product of a metonymic process in which the contiguity of fragments (planets mixed with countries and companies) has more impact on our perception of reality than the full display of the situations to which these fragments belong. Countries were commodified while corporations were raised to the status of planets. This peculiar transformation, sponsored by the growing internationalization of consumption, may be seen as the start of the highly volatile process in which signs are now fully engaged. Such commodification also implied the wholesale marketing of progress as efficiency: measured by the extent of its range—the most exotic countries, the remotest planets—progress became equivalent to speed and minimum effort.[13]

In the metaphor of an illuminated humanity, the conquest of space can be seen as the last Romantic dream. What else, if not the extreme of romantic longing, could explain the space age's total investment in the good of progress, based on the firm belief that human control over matter would result in a better society?[14] Yet this universe of progress was doomed to rust like Brasília, the city of the future built in the late 1950s to be Brazil's capital. Designed in 1957 by architect Oscar Niemayer and inaugurated in 1960, Brasília is one of two contemporary cities raised from scratch. Instead of evolving from a previous urban foundation, Brasília was built in a deserted area in the middle of Brazil so that it could function as the bureaucratic heart of that vast country and its segregated regions. Conceived as the city of the future (André Malraux called it "the capital of hope"), it was the utopian dream come true: orderly, efficient, fully controlled. A witness to the fate of modernity, Brasília now stands as an isolated and decaying giant consumed by the enormous bureaucratic apparatus that gave it life, a gloomy scenario akin to that in the film *Brazil* (Terry Gilliam, 1985). Like other bureaucratic cities—Washington, D.C., for instance—it is a place of transition, crossed by lawyers and diplomats who stay for a few years: only its service population is relatively stable. Nobody goes there dreaming of the future anymore.

Similarly, the two remaining monuments of the 1964-65 World's Fair stand as sad witnesses of the decline of progress. The Unisphere, once a symbol of universal outreach, is now used as a swimming pool by crowds who are oblivious to the giant's past glory; the New York State Pavilion's "Tent of Tomorrow" survives as a few rusty wires, the blown-up map of New York state that served as its skating rink covered with stagnant water and weeds. Entire fair sites, like that of Expo '67 in Montreal, have been abandoned to the fate of time. Modernity's disdain for the past ignored the possibility of a newness that could turn obsolete overnight. In retrospect, the exhilarated space age was a swan song for the dream of the future. Consistently, what remains of it are decaying structures—the abandoned skeletons of aerial cities and world's fairs that languished awaiting a future that never arrived.[15]

Science Fiction; or, Fearing the Body Snatchers

As technological development grew, so did the fear of its consequences, producing contradictory notions of progress and degeneration, belief in the future and anxiety over self-destruction. The ability to decompose and reconstruct the human organism, to reach faraway planets, and to destroy entire cities produced mixed feelings that undermined the constitution of a cultural identity based on the notion of scientific pragmatism. Consequently, space age fears centered on the body as the most vulnerable and threatened site, establishing a clear dichotomy between body and mind. Nowhere is this better expressed than in one of the most popular genres of the period, science fiction films. In the classic *Forbidden Planet* (Fred McLeod Wilcox, 1956) a space crew arrives on a planet where a scientist, accompanied by his sexy daughter and their servant robot, guards the secret of the planet's former inhabitants: an advanced society that attained a remarkable degree of civilization but disappeared mysteriously. A double narrative unfolds: the daughter's sexual awakening (unfolding through multiple dress changes) and the all-male crew pressing the father to explain both the achievements and the disappearance of the vanished civilization. To everybody's terror, the crew begins to vanish in the hands of enormous, colorful, and furious energy forces—none other than "the monsters of the id," the repressed unconscious forces of a civilization that made the fatal mistake of trusting only its conscious progress.

The exploration of the human body's frontiers was put forth by the 1950s and 1960s science fiction movies as apocalyptic fantasies of invasions from other planets, genetic deformations, and gigantic animals that could gobble down all of humanity in a few hours. Usually attributed to Cold War paranoia (the American fear of a communist invasion) and postwar feelings of perishability, the fear was mainly articulated as anxiety over becoming inhuman. This obsession with physical or psychological transformation has now resurfaced in both the current cult status of some of these films and the fact that they are often being remade. Two examples among several are *The Fly* (Kurt Neumann, 1958; David Cronenberg, 1986), in which genetic transformation punishes

Dichotomy between body and mind? Film still from *Forbidden Planet*, directed by Fred McLeod Wilcox, 1956. Courtesy the Museum of Modern Art/Film Stills Archive.

scientific experiment in a man whose body is partly transmuted into that of a fly's, and *The Invasion of the Body Snatchers* (Don Siegel, 1956; Philip Kaufman, 1978), in which beings from outer space take over human bodies, reproducing them void of any feelings.

To counter this threat to humanity, people of both the space age and the postmodern age have attempted to imagine themselves as characters from another time, belonging either to the future or to the past and hoping to retain a sense of identity through that vicarious experience. Yet the irony of this schizophrenic exchanging of identities is that vicariousness is the ability to become, however fleetingly, another— exactly what the fear of dehumanization tries so hard to avoid. Films like *Back to the Future* (Robert Zemeckis, 1985) and *Peggy Sue Got Married* (Francis Ford Coppola, 1986) show the extent of this melancholic desire's repetitive compulsiveness. In *Back to the Future,* the main character goes back in time to the moment right before his parents got engaged. In a highly oedipal narrative, his mother falls in love with him and he has to create a complicated series of diversions to convince her to marry his father instead. In *Peggy Sue Got Married,*

Peggy Sue reverts to her adolescence, living out the fantasy of marrying her girlhood beau. In both cases, the leap is of about three decades, placing the characters in the late 1950s. Such a regression suggests an acute denial of the self: not only is the future wiped out, the present is replaced by the past and thus declared nonexistent. Furthermore, returning to the moment a family is constituted implies a desire for structure and hierarchy, suggesting that the retro fashion's melancholy has much to do with wanting a stricter and more rigid ideology, a desire consistent with the conservative backlash of the 1980s.

It is worth noting, although the implications are beyond the scope of this chapter, that science fiction films' portrayal of the fears of bodily harm explicitly present the female body as a threat. Since the space age is, after all, the fantasy of *man's* dominion over nature, women are portrayed as competing with extraterrestrials and gigantic spiders in monstrosity, the only difference being that the woman's is a monstrosity always connected to sexuality. The most famous low-budget film of the genre, *Attack of the 50-foot Woman* (Nathan Juran, 1958), for example, transfigures a betrayed wife into a huge and vengeful Valkyrie who crushes the unfaithful one in her clutch. This fear is analogically reenacted in a later version of the struggle between nature and technology: *Alien* (Ridley Scott, 1979). In *Alien,* technology is invaded by an animal form whose most outstanding feature is an unbridled fertility. In a fatal phallic/uterine insertion, the alien engenders its children in human bodies, as the film, exacerbating its male paranoia, slowly gets rid of the men in charge of the spaceship. *Alien* presents terror of reproduction as the conflict of two irreconcilable motherhoods, one primitive (organic) and annihilating, the other modern (technological) and absent, one excessively prolific, the other sterile.

The Space Age as a Parodic Souvenir

It is this extremely contradictory period, in which human beings simultaneously see themselves mastering the laws of the universe and obsessively recreating the threat of self-annihilation, to which a certain postmodern trend looks back in admiration. However aware we may be of the second-degree quality of the space age comeback, the melancholy quality of this personification is made apparent by the paradox of having to pilfer a sense of future from the past. We revert to the years in which the fantasy of how our time would be was being formulated.

While in the 1950s and 1960s imaginary projections were thrust toward the near future, in the 1980s the failure of the futuristic dream has led to reappropriation and recycling of the moment when the dream was enunciated.

It is therefore not a coincidence that the two most conspicuous sub-cultures involved in the retro fashion are children of the baby-boomer era: yuppies and young gay men.[16] Despite important differences, these groups, both mainly white, middle class, and in their late twenties and early thirties, have more in common than meets the eye: their delight in recycling the 1950s and 1960s seems to be born out of two modes of sign homogenization that produce a similar outcome. Known for their conservative, materialistic outlook, yuppies (young urban professionals) are intent on reproducing the nuclear family paradigm with the professional female as the only twist. Determined by exchange value, yuppie subculture homogenizes everything for easy consumption. Consistently, yuppies are the sponsors and most important patrons of the current "ethnic pop" fad in clothes, food, and music, in which difference is not an attribute but rather a source of entertainment. This kind of ethnic diversity is but an extension of the homogenization that occurs in high technology: all signs are equivalent and therefore basically, although not ultimately, interchangeable.[17]

While yuppies use money as a means of neutralizing difference, many young gay men use their bodies as a celebratory means of camouflage and absorption of difference. Rather than the explicit transvestism of drag—characteristic of the previous gay generation and its coming-out boldness—these men are prone to the more contained neo-Romantic or neo-punk looks, the body as the territory on which infinite characters and personas can be explored on a daily basis. The body becomes a ship that can sail fluidly through different times and places, always moving and changing, adapting to each port of call but anchoring nowhere.[18] Money and body alike, then, serve as conduits for the circulation of signs, enabling a swift exchange void of the weight of referentiality. It is not a history or a peculiar culture that is being referred to in this way of quoting, it is rather an iconographic richness that is being happily cannibalized. Such anthropophagic pleasure is underscored by its explicit artificiality. These personifications are lived theatrically, apparently without emotional investment, but with a fascination for artificiality itself.

The more blatantly iconographic and staged, the more cardboard-like the images used, the better. Which is why space age retro—with its overdetermination of meaning (where icons are so many versions of the notion of progress), its intensely figurative quality, its saturated colors, and its attempts to transform all the surrounding space into one huge movie set—is so attractive to postmodern culture. The current recirculation of B movies illustrates the attraction of artificiality. These low-budget films, which proliferated during the 1950s and 1960s, were characterized by their makeshift sets and by the explicitness of a narrative that had to unfold in as few locations as possible. Their cheapness of production was compensated by an excessive melodrama. Titles like *It! The Terror from Beyond Space* (Edward L. Cahn, 1958) and *Sins of the Fleshapoids* (Mike Cuchar, 1965) are among today's most sought-after cult films. So are the special-effects films like *Cat Women of the Moon* (Arthur Hilton, 1953), in 3-D, and *The Tingler* (William Castle, 1959) and its use of "percepto," a small electric shock administered to the audience at appropriate moments, "unleash[ing] the insectlike TINGLER right onto the spinal cords of the terrified audience."[19]

This artificiality is further highlighted by the films' abundant use of secondhand footage. Anticipating the current recycling of all available imagery, the space age did not hesitate for one moment to use what it needed for effect: if it couldn't be filmed within the production budget, it was stolen from somewhere else. This is the case in one of the most terrifying and beautiful of all sci-fi films: *The War of the Worlds* (Byron Haskin, 1953). Here, Earth is invaded by a legion of swanlike spaceships that destroy everything with their powerful beams. World War II footage illustrates the devastation: in mesmerizing scenes, rows of buildings lie in smoking heaps and the musical score is punctuated with silent pauses. Once Earth's inhabitants have given up all hope, the alien ships, their destructive mission almost complete, begin to collapse. The aliens are defeated by Earth's common cold, a defeat that is scarcely a relief. Instead, their deaths add more sadness to a film in which very little survives.

Alternately exuding happiness and distress over the advancement of technology, the films and television programs mentioned here seldom question this ambivalence explicitly, choosing rather to indulge in the ecstasy or the terror. Yet it is precisely the combination of such hardly believable naiveté and intense emotionality that makes these productions so much more unreal and therefore appealing to a sensibility that finds in artificiality the articulation of its own conflictive affect. Artificiality, then, covers the emptiness opened up by the perceptual gap with a world saturated in the most explicit allusiveness. Whereas high tech seeks efficiency and condensation, promoting a cold, controlled, electronic universe, space age retro provides the melancholic parody of that world: an unambiguous spectacle of people whose motivations can be read without difficulty, whose emotions are so extreme that they become melodramatic, and whose scenarios are overfilled to such an extent that they can only be fake. By opposing figuration to digitalization and iconography to absence, space age retro becomes a continuing soap opera of high technology, allowing our culture a much-needed detachment and perspective. For all its homogenization of times and situations, space age retro enables us to take a humorous look at our fears.

Ironically, space age iconography has helped two eras to channel their fears: the 1950s and 1960s by countering dehumanization with monsters, aliens, and a perfect future; postmodernity by offering these same metaphors as a bleak parody of the threat of technology, something contemporary culture scarcely dares to face. In this light, the recycling of whole periods appears as much more than a vacuous repetition, product of either a supposed lack of creativity or an insatiable consumption. On the contrary, it becomes a practical way of culturally coping with otherwise inexpressible conflicts. To a cynical postmodernity, so aware of the rise and fall of cultures, ideologies, and movements, to manifest an ambivalent relationship to technology is a necessary, however fantastic, exit.

That this happens through others' fantasies is only consistent with a culture whose detached perception, as I suggested earlier, impedes direct experience. Far from viewing the 1950s and 1960s nostalgically, as a golden age now forever gone—which is usually the case with comeback trends and utopian visions, in which the present is abandoned in favor of either past or future—the contemporary attachment to space age iconography is both humorously distant and utterly melancholic: it denies that iconography's mortality yet lives it as a second-hand parody. In this way, the 1950s and 1960s are emptied of historicity in favor of their synchronic attributes: the concrete, spatial remains of the dream of progress. Decontextualized, these remains become full-fledged allegories, their connection to the period in which they were produced acritical and unimportant. As fragments, they can be reproduced at any given time strictly for their surface value, always unfolding in the present.

It is in this sense that melancholia opposes souvenirs to corpses: while corpses still undergo a process of decay and deterioration, sou-

venirs are instant ruins: they freeze a moment in time, avoiding progression altogether.[20] As its uncontrollable iconography shows, the
space age was already dead at its onset. Otherwise, it would not have
needed to represent itself so compulsively, seeking in imagery the cer-
tainty it lacked. Unwittingly, the space age was setting itself up to be a
wonderful scenario devoid of chronological anchorage—thus its comfortable renaissance in the 1980s. The space age's ambition to control
space was in fact a way of struggling against being lost in its own
space, an attempt to find in the imaginary conquest of other planets
and temporal dimensions a sense of location it longed for. Anticipating
today's psychasthenic fusion with imagery, the space age created an
entire universe to hide in.

Between a future in ruins and a past that is but a costume for another
personification, contemporary culture is stuck in an allegorical present,
unable to return nostalgically to the past or advance hopefully into the
future. In the struggle between allegory and symbol, intrinsically related to the struggle of identity (who and how to be in the world), space
and body act as metaphors in the reformulation of cultural identity. Ag-
gravated by the massive proliferation of technological imagery, the
contiguity of space and body leads to the blending of image and self:
it is virtually impossible to distinguish the "original" 1950s from the recycled version, which is constituted by vicariousness to such an extreme degree that the boundaries between past, present, and future
are rendered useless and nominal.

In many senses, the space age is a metaphor for the built-in cadu-
city of modernity. In its desire to be rooted in the present, modernity
despised everything that came before it as old-fashioned and obsolete. Yet, since modernity was in fact vulnerable to the passing of time,
this denial could only backfire by leaving it no temporal respite. As contradictory as technology's fast obsolescence, modernity's aging—
already a past in the present—could only find in space a place to exist.
Incapable of being history, modernity could only be a ruin. It is in the
paradoxes of a deteriorated future, of a belief born out of disappointment, of an emptiness satiated by icons, that the space age and postmodernity meet: one looking forward, the other backward; one living in
a fantasy, the other living another's fantasy; one within the debris of
wars, the other within the debris of dreams. It is this quality of permanently living at a second remove that underlies our time, raising it to an
almost artistic level of detachment—hence its inevitable fascination
with the baroque and the decadent.

Three

Holy Kitschen
Collecting Religious
Junk from the Street

*Kitsch causes two tears to flow in quick
succession. The first tear says: How nice to see
children running on the grass! The second tear
says: How nice to be moved, together with all
mankind, by children running on the grass! It is
the second tear that makes kitsch kitsch.*
Milan Kundera, 1984

Catholic imagery, once confined to sacred places such as church
souvenir stands, cemeteries, and botanicas, has recently invaded the
market as a fad. In the last few years, the realm of religious iconography in Manhattan has extended beyond its traditional Latino outlets on
the Lower East Side, the Upper West Side, and Fourteenth Street. The
1980s appropriation of an imagery that evokes transcendence illustrates the cannibalistic and vicarious characteristics of postmodern
culture. This melancholic arrogation also diffuses the boundaries of
cultural identity and difference, producing a new and unsettling cultural persona.

A walk along Fourteenth Street used to be enough to travel in the
hyperreality of kitsch iconography.[1] Cutting across the map of Manhattan, Fourteenth Street sets the boundary for downtown, exploding into
a frontierlike bazaar, a frantic place of trade and exchange, a truly in-
ner-city port where among cascades of plastic flowers, pelicans made
with shells, rubber shoes, Rita Hayworth towels, two-dollar digital
watches, and pink electric guitars with miniature microphones, an ar-
ray of shrine furnishings is offered. Velvet hangings picturing the Last
Supper are flanked on one side by bucolic landscapes where young
couples kiss as the sun fizzles away in the ocean and on the other by
1987's "retro" idol, Elvis Presley, while the Virgin Mary's golden aura is
framed by the sexy legs of a pin-up, and the Sacred Heart of Jesus

St. Theresa with Starfish Halo, Photo copyright Dana Salvo, Chiapas, Mexico, 1989.

desperately competes in glitter with barrages of brightly colored glass-bead curtains.[2]

Nowadays, the Catholic iconography brought to the United States by immigrants from Puerto Rico, the Dominican Republic, Mexico, and Cuba is displayed in places where the predominant attitude toward Latino culture is one of amused fascination. Religious images serve not only as memorabilia in fancy souvenir shops[3] but also as decoration for night clubs. The now-exorcised Voodoo, on Eighteenth Street, used to have a disco on its first floor and a bright green and pink tropical bar on the second. The bar's ceiling was garnished with plastic fruits hanging from one end to the other, and in the center of the room stood an altar complete with Virgin Mary, flowers, and votive candles. Fourteenth Street's Palladium, famous for a postmodern scenario in which golden Renaissance paintings emerge from behind a bare high-tech structure, celebrated All Saints' Day in 1987 with an invitation that unfolded in images of and prayers to Saint Patrick, Saint Francis of Assisi, and Saint Michael the Archangel.

Suddenly, holiness is all over the place. For $3.25 one can buy a Holiest Water Fountain in the shape of the Virgin, while plastic fans engraved with the images of your favorite holy people go for $1.95, as do Catholic identification tags: "I'm a Catholic. In case of accident or illness please call a priest." Glowing rosary beads can be found for $1.25 and, for those in search of verbal illustration, a series of "Miniature Stories of the Saints" is available for only $1.45. In the wake of punk crucifix earrings comes designer Henry Auvil's Sacred Heart of Jesus sweatshirt, yours for a modest eighty dollars,[4] while scapularies, sometimes brought all the way from South America, adorn black leather jackets. Even John Paul II has something to contribute. In his travels, the Holy Father leaves behind a trail of images, and one can buy his smiling face in a variety of pope gadgets including alarm clocks, pins, picture frames, T-shirts, and snowstorm globes.[5]

This holy invasion has gone so far as to intrude in the sacred space of galleries and museums, as a growing number of artists incorporate Catholic religious imagery in their work. Some recent examples are Amalia Mesa-Bains's recasting of personal *altares,* Dana Salvo's photographs of Mexican home altars, and Audrey Flack's baroque re-representations of Spanish virgins.[6] Can the objects found in botanicas and on Fourteenth Street, the ones sold in souvenir shops and those exhibited in galleries be considered one and the same? I will argue for their synchronized difference, that is, for contemporary urban culture's ability to circulate and support distinct, and often contradictory, discourses.

Religious Iconography as Kitsch: Developing a Vicarious Sensibility

I will begin by describing the peculiar aesthetics and philosophy underlying the circulation of the iconography of home altars. A popular Latin American tradition, home altars or *altares* are domestic spaces dedicated to deities and holy figures. In them, statuettes or images of virgins and saints are allocated space together with candles and other votive objects. Triangular in analogy to the Holy Trinity, *altares* are characterized by a cluttered juxtaposition of all types of paraphernalia; they are a personal pastiche. Illustrating a history of wishes, laments, and prayers, they are built over time, each personal incident leaving its own mark. *Altares* embody familiar or individual histories in the way photo albums do for some people. Consequently, a home altar is not only unique and unrepeatable, it is coded by the personal experience that composed it, and the code is unreadable to foreign eyes. This mode of elaboration explains the variety of artifacts to be found in home altars and why there are no set rules as to what they might be made up of, except that everything must have a particular value. In *altares,* value is measured both sentimentally and as an offering. Since most of the people who make them have low incomes, their economic worth is symbolic and is conveyed by glitter and shine, mirrors and glass, a profusion of golden and silvery objects, and sheer abundance. This symbolic richness accounts for the artificial look of *altares,* as well as for the "magical kingdom" feeling they evoke.

Fundamentally syncretic, *altares* are raised or dedicated to figures who are public in some way, usually taken from the Catholic tradition, a local miraculous event, or national politics. Instead of following a formal chronology, home altars rearticulate history in relation to events relevant to the believer. To symbolize personal history, they transgress boundaries of time, space, class, and race. This is well illustrated in the Venezuelan cult of María Lionza, a deity who is revered along with heroes of the Independence and contemporary presidents—such as Carlos Andrés Pérez—in the gigantic altar of Sorte, a ritual hill dedicated to her worship. In both their elaboration and their meaning, *altares* are emblematic of the mechanics of popular culture: they familiarize transcendental experience by creating a personal universe from mainly domestic resources. In so doing, they stand directly opposite the impersonal politics of high and mass culture, although they steal motifs and objects from both.

That the *altares* tradition is being appropiated by artists both in the United States and abroad (Cuban artist Leandro Soto's home altars to revolutionary heroes, for example) at the same time that their constitutive elements are heavily circulated in the marketplace is no coincidence. This phenomenon is based on the stealing of elements that are foreign or removed from the absorbing culture's direct sensory realm, shaping itself into a vicarious experience particularly attracted to the intensity of feeling provided by iconographic universes like that of Latin American Catholicism. Vicariousness—to live through another's experience—is a fundamental trait of postmodern culture. Ethnicity and cultural difference have exchanged their intrinsic values for the more extrinsic ones of market interchangeability: gone are the times when people could make a persuasive claim to a culture of their own, a set of meaningful practices that might be considered the product of unique thought or lifestyle. The new sense of time and space generated by telecommunications—in the substitution of continuity and distance with instantaneousness and ubiquity—has transformed the perception of things so that they are no longer lived directly but through their representations. Experience is mainly available through signs: things are not lived directly but rather through the agency of a medium, in the consumption of images and objects that replace what they stand for. Such rootlessness accounts for the high volatility and ultimate transferability of culture in postmodern times.

The imaginary participation that occurs in vicarious experience is often despised for its lack of pertinence to what is tacitly agreed upon as reality, for example in the generalized notion that mass entertainment is dumbfounding. Ironically enough, vicariousness is similar to the classic understanding of aesthetic enjoyment, which is founded on a symbolically distanced relationship to phenomena. This symbolic connection, which used to protect the exclusivity of aesthetic experience by basing it on the prerequisites of trained sensibility and knowledge, has given way to the more ordinary and accessible passageway provided by popular culture. Therefore, it is not against living others' experiences—or living like another—that high-culture criticisms are directed, but rather against the popular level where this vicariousness is acted out and the repercussions it has on other cultural projects. Vicariousness is acceptable so long as it involves a high-level project (stimulating the intellect) but unacceptable when limited to the sensory (stimulating the senses).

The acceptance of vicariousness enables an understanding of how, as the result of a long cultural process, simulation has come to occupy the place of a traditional, indexical referentiality. For this process is not, as many would have it, the sole responsibility of progressively sophisticated media and market devices, but is rather the radicalization of the ways in which culture has always mediated our experience. The difference in postmodernity is both quantitative and qualitative, since it lies in the extent to which experience is lived vicariously as well as in the centrality of emotion to contemporary vicariousness. The "waning of affect" in contemporary culture that I discussed in the prologue is intrinsically related to a distance from immediate experience caused in part by the current emphasis on signs.[7] Attempting to compensate for emotional detachment, this sensibility continually searches for intense thrills and for the acute emotionality attributed to other times and peoples. The homogenization of signs and the wide circulation of marketable goods make all cultures susceptible to this appropriation, and the more imbued with emotional intensity they.are perceived to be, the better. It is in this appeal to emotion that religious imagery and kitsch converge. The connection proves particularly relevant because kitsch permits the articulation of the polemics of high and low culture in a context broader than that of religious imagery, smoothing the way for a better understanding of its attraction and importance for vicarious experience.

Known as the domain of "bad taste," kitsch stands for artistic endeavor gone sour as well as for anything that is considered too obvious, dramatic, repetitive, artificial, or exaggerated. The link between religious imagery and kitsch is based on the dramatic character of their styles, whose function is to evoke unambiguously, dispelling ambivalence and abstraction. After all, besides providing a meaningful frame for existence and allocating emotions and feelings, Catholicism facilitates through its imagery the materialization of one of the most ungraspable of all experiences, that of the transcendence of spiritual attributes. Because of the spiritual nature of religious faith, however, iconolatry (the worship of images or icons) is often seen as sacrilegious, as the vulgarization of an experience that should remain fundamentally immaterial and ascetic. In this sense, not only Catholic iconography but the whole of Christian theology has been accused of lacking in substance, and therefore of being irredeemably kitsch.[8] Like kitsch, religious imagery is a mise-en-scène, a visual glossolalia that embodies otherwise impalpable qualities: mystic fervor is translated into upturned eyes, a gaping mouth, and levitation; goodness always feeds white sheep; virginity is surrounded by auras, clouds, and smiling cherubim; passion is a bleeding heart; and evil is snakes, horns, and flames. In kitsch, this dramatic quality is intensified by an overtly sentimental, melodramatic tone and by primary colors and bright, glossy surfaces.

The crossing over between the spheres of the celestial and kitsch is truly concordant. Religious imagery is considered kitsch because of its desacralization, while kitsch is called evil and the "anti-Christ in art"[9] because of its artistic profanities. Kitsch steals motifs and materials at random, regardless of the original ascription of the sources. It takes from classic, modernist, and popular art and mixes all together, becoming in this way the first and foremost recycler. This irreverent eclecticism has brought both glory and doom upon kitsch, for its unbridled voraciousness transgresses boundaries and undermines hierarchies. Religious kitsch is then doubly irreverent, displaying an impious overdetermination that accounts, perhaps, for its secular seduction.

Kitsch is one of the constitutive phenomena of postmodernism. The qualities attributed so far to kitsch—eclectic cannibalism, recycling, re-

joicing in surface or allegorical values—are those that distinguish contemporary sensibility from the previous belief in authenticity, originality,
and symbolic depth.[10] Furthermore, the postmodern broadening of the
notion of reality, whereby vicariousness is no longer felt as false or secondhand but rather as an autonomous, however incredible, dimension
of the real, facilitates the current circulation and revalorization of this
aesthetics. Likewise, in its chaotic juxtaposition of images and times,
contemporary urban culture is comparable to an altarlike reality, where
the logic of organization is anything but homogeneous, visual saturation is obligatory, and the personal is lived as a pastiche of fragmented
images from popular culture.

Fourteenth Street and First-Degree Kitsch

One of the most conspicuous features of postmodernity is its ability to
entertain conflicting discourses simultaneously. Rather than erasing
previous practices, it enables and even seeks their subsistence. This
peculiar coexistence of divergent visions is made possible by the
space left in the vertical displacement of depth by surface, which implies a gathering on the horizontal level. Fragmentary but ubiquitous,
discontinuous and instantaneous, this new altarlike reality is the arena
for a Byzantine struggle in which different iconographies fight for hegemony. In this manner, cultural specificity has given way to the internationalization of its signs, losing uniqueness and gaining exposure
and circulation. Within this context, it is possible to distinguish, according to their means of production and cultural function, three degrees of
kitsch that have recently come to overlap in time and space.

In what I will call first-degree kitsch, representation is based on an
indexical referent. Here, the difference between reality and representation is explicit and hierarchical, since only what is perceived as reality
matters. Acting as a mere substitute, the kitsch object has no validity in
and of itself.[11] This is the case of the imagery available at church en-
trances and botanicas, sold for its straightforward iconic value. Statuettes, images, and scapularies embody the spirits they represent, making them palpable. Consequently, this imagery belongs in sacred
places, such as home altars, and must be treated with utmost respect.
In first-degree kitsch, the relationship between object and user is immediate, one of genuine belief. Technically, its production is simple
and cheap, a serial artisanship devoid of that perfectly finished look
attained with a more sophisticated technology.[12] In fact, these objects

exhibit a certain rawness that is, or appears to be, handmade. This quality reflects their "honesty," as lack of sophistication is usually taken for authenticity. On the other hand, this rawness adds to first-degree kitsch's status as "low" art, when it is considered art at all: usually, if not marginalized as folklore, it is condemned as gaudy.[13]

Almost a century old, first-degree kitsch is what is usually referred to in discussions of kitsch. It is not, however, inherently kitsch. It is understood as such from a more distanced look, one that does not enjoy the same emotional attachment that believers have to these objects. For them, kitsch objects are meaningful, even when they are used ornamentally. Yet for those who have the distanced look, whom I will call kitsch aficionados,[14] it is precisely this unintentionality that is attractive, since it speaks of a naive immediacy of feeling that they have lost. Aficionados' nostalgia leads them to a vicarious pleasure that gratifies their desire for immediacy. They achieve this pleasure by collecting kitsch objects and even admiring their inherent qualities: bright colors, glossy surfaces, and figuration. By elaborating a scenario for their vicarious pleasure, kitsch aficionados paradoxically reproduce the practice of believers, since this scenario is meant to provide an otherwise unattainable experience, that of immediate feeling for the aficionados and of reverence for the believers. Aficionados' sensibility cannot be dismissed as secondary or intellectual because their attachment to these objects is as strong and vital as that of first-degree believers. Yet what is relevant here is that first-degree believers' attachment is directly related to the devotional meaning of the iconography, while for aficionados, this meaning is secondary: what matters is not what the images represent, but the intense feelings — hope, fear, awe — that they inspire. Aficionados' connection is to these emotions, their appreciation one step removed from first-degree kitsch.

The different relationships to first-degree kitsch may be illustrated by a Fourteenth Street fad of the past few years, the Christ clocks. Rectangular or circular, these clocks narrate various moments of Christ's life in three dimensions. We see Christ gently blessing a blond girl while a few small, fluffy white sheep watch reverently, Christ bleeding on the cross or delivering the Sermon on the Mount, or all of these scenes together in the special "quarter-hour" versions, where, in the narrative logic of the Stations of the Cross, each quarter hour has its own episode. True to Fourteenth Street and home-altar aesthetics, Christ clocks eschew the boredom of bareness, naturalness, and discretion and exploit the prurience of loudness, dramatics, and sentimentality.

New York City's Fourteenth Street.

The profusion of these clocks bears witness to their popularity. Selling for about twelve to fourteen dollars, they have become a dominant part of the Fourteenth Street scene.

For most Christ-clock shoppers there is no contradiction in using Christ's life as a backdrop for time. In kitchens or living rooms, these clocks are used as extensions of the home altar, conveying a comfortable familiarity with a figure that represents cherished values. This relationship to Christ is loving and quotidian, totally ordinary. For kitsch aficionados, however, these clocks are a source of endless amazement and wonder. Lacking a religious attachment to them, aficionados are fascinated by the directness of the feelings these clocks represent and evoke: there is something definitely moving about Christ's sorrow as—on his knees on Mount Olive, hands dramatically clasped—he implores his Father's compassion for the sinful human race. For an aficionado it is the intensity of this drama—heightened by an artificial aura created by the picture's lack of depth and bright colors—that is attractive. This aesthetic experience is radically different from the highly conceptualized one of modern art.

Little Rickie and Second-Degree Kitsch

First-degree kitsch familiarizes the ungraspable—eternity, goodness, evil—while tacitly maintaining a hierarchical distinction between reality and representation. The opposite is true of second-degree kitsch, or neo-kitsch,[15] which collapses this difference by making representation into the only possible referent. In so doing, it defamiliarizes our notion of reality because representation itself becomes the real. Neo-kitsch is inspired by first-degree kitsch and is therefore second-generation. Sold as kitsch, it lacks the devotional relation present in first-degree kitsch. Its absence of feeling leaves us with an empty icon, or rather an icon whose value lies precisely in its iconicity, its quality as a sign rather than as an object. This kitsch is self-referential—a sort of kitsch-kitsch—and has lost all the innocence and charm of the first-degree experience.

Whereas first-degree kitsch is sold in variety stores, among articles of domestic use, second-degree kitsch is found in more specialized shops, like those that sell souvenirs. Among the most interesting is New York's Little Rickie, where in the midst of all types of memorabilia, religious imagery reigns. In its dizzying clutteredness, Little Rickie is a sophisticated microcosm of Fourteenth Street and home-altar aesthetics. As such, it succeeds in creating a total disorientation that engulfs the viewer inside the store. But although it offers all the religious kitsch one could ever hope to find, the catch for aficionados lies in the given or prefabricated quality of the objects. Take for instance the holy water bottles, transparent plastic bottles in the shape of the Virgin Mary. These bottles stand obliquely to the original iconography—which does not include them—and rely exclusively on concept for their existence. Lacking in visual and signifying exuberance, they profit from the religious imagery fad and from the idea of a bottle for holy water being funny. Never having established a first degree of affection, these bottles are devoid of the intensity aficionados seek. They are simply toys, curiosities bought to show or give to somebody else. Second-degree kitsch exists only for transaction, to pass from hand to hand, and in this lack of possessing subject lies its ultimate alienation and perishability.

Neo-kitsch is intentional, and it capitalizes on an acquired taste for tackiness. It is a popularization of the camp sensibility, a perspective wherein appreciation of the "ugly" conveys to the spectator an aura of refined decadence, an ironic enjoyment from a position of enlightened superiority.[16] This attitude allows a safe release into sentimentality. Neo-kitsch's exchange value is intensified by the interchangeability of religious imagery with the rest of the memorabilia in the store. For consumers of second-degree kitsch, the choice between, say, a sample of holy soil and a plastic eye with two feet that winks as it walks around is totally arbitrary, decided only by last-minute caprice or a vague idea of which would be more hilarious. For "authentic" aficionados half the pleasure of acquisition is lost when kitsch is a given and not a discovery. As for first-degree believers, they are not among the store's buyers, although the store is located in the East Village, which is home to a substantial Latino community.

Mass marketed, these products involve a more elaborate technology and often come from mass-culture production centers like Hong Kong. First-degree homeyness is replaced by the mechanical look of serial reproduction. Designed as a commodity for exchange and commerce, second-degree kitsch has no trace of use value, no longer being "the real thing" for connoisseurs. The passing over of kitsch to mass culture is similar to the desacralization of high art occasioned by mechanical reproduction.[17] In both cases the loss of authenticity is based on the shift from manufactured or low-technology production to a more sophisticated industrial one, with its consequent displacement of a referent for a copy. To consider second-degree kitsch less authentic than first-degree kitsch because of its predigested character would be contradictory, since kitsch is by definition predigested. The difference lies in how intentional, or self-conscious, this predigestion is.

The mass marketing of religious imagery as kitsch is only possible once the icon has been stripped of its signifying value. The religious kitsch that was available before the 1980s was first-degree kitsch, albeit mechanically reproduced. The change to a fad, something fun to play with, is a recent phenomenon. What matters now is iconicity itself; worth is measured by the icon's traits—the formal, technical aspects like narrative, color, and texture. Void, except in a nostalgic way, of the systemic meaning granted by religious belief, these traits are easily isolated and fragmented, becoming totally interchangeable and metonymical. As floating signs, they can adhere to any object and convey onto it their full value, "kitschifying" it. This lack of specificity accounts for neo-kitsch objects' suitability for random consumption.

Third-Degree Kitsch and the Advantages of Recycling

Religious imagery reached its highest level of commodification when it lost specificity to market interchangeability. It has gained a new social place, however, thanks to a simultaneous and related process: the legitimization of its signifying and visual attributes by the institutionally

Angel of the Asphalt, calendar print circa 1954.
Copyright The Ken Brown collection, Ken Brown
Cards, 1988.

authorized agency of artists. This revaluation takes place through the multifarious recycling of Catholic religious iconography, constituting what I will distinguish as third-degree kitsch. Here, the iconography is invested with either a new or a foreign set of meanings, generating a hybrid product. This phenomenon is the outcome of the blending between Latin and North American cultures and includes both Chicano and Nuyorican artists' recovery of their heritage as well as white American artists working with the elements of this tradition.

Since individual *altares* represent personal histories of memories and wishes, the tradition of home altars as a whole can be taken to represent collective remembrance and desire. In varying degrees of nostalgia and transformation, several Chicano and Nuyorican artists are using the *altares* format to reaffirm a precarious sense of belonging. Second-generation altar making is complicated by the currency of its iconography: in more ways than one, the fashionable home altars' aesthetic benefits from such timely recirculation. Yet any consideration of these artists as the authentic bearers of the *altares* tradition assures

Chicano and Nuyorican artists' marginality by stating that they are the most suited to carry on with their forebears' work, since cultural continuity conveniently eliminates them from participating in other creative endeavors. Chicano and Nuyorican home altar recycling, therefore, is treading a very fine line between reelaborating a tradition whose exclusive rights are questionable and being artistically identified solely with that task.

Some of the edge can be taken off this discussion by acknowledging the differences between this kind of artistic recovery and first-degree home-altar elaboration. As a recent exhibition title suggests, the recasting of *altares* is often meant as a "ceremony of memory" that invests them with a new political signification and awareness. This artistic legitimization implies formalizing home altars to fit into a system of meaning where they represent the culture that once was; they are changed, once again, from referents to signs. This loss of innocence, however, allows *altares* to be reelaborated into new sets of meanings, many of which were inconceivable to the original bearers of this tradition but are certainly fundamental to more recent Chicano and Nuyorican generations.[18]

One such example of home-altar recycling may be found in Amalia Mesa-Bains's work, which is both a recovery of and a challenge to her family tradition and cultural identity. Mesa-Bains is a Chicana who began making *altares* after earning several college degrees. Her revival of this tradition is therefore not spontaneous but calculated, impelled by a conscious gesture of political reaffirmation of Chicano cultural values. One of her recent shows, Grotto of the Virgin, consisted of *altares* raised to such unhallowed figures as Mexican painter Frida Kahlo, Mexican superstar Dolores del Rio, and her own grandmother. What is specific to Mesa-Bains's altars is that the personal is not subordinated to a particular holy person. Rather, a secular person is made sacred by the altar format, the offerings consisting mainly of a reconstruction of that person's imagined life by means of images and gadgets. The Dolores del Rio altar, for example, is raised on several steps made with mirrors, bringing to mind the image cults that grow up around Hollywood actors and actresses. This altar is stacked with feminine paraphernalia such as perfume bottles, lipstick, and jewelry, as well as letters, pictures, and other souvenirs of her life. In this way, the image of Dolores del Rio as a "cinema goddess" becomes literal.

This secularization of the *altares* is probably due to the importance Mesa-Bains assigns to personal experience. In traditional altar raising, the personal was always secondary to the deity, and religious sensibility articulated in the last instance the whole altar. By privileging what were only coding elements so that they become the main objective of her *altares,* Mesa-Bains has inverted the traditional formula. As a result, women and mass culture are invested with a new power that emanates from the sacredness of *altares:* in postmodern culture, Mesa-Bains's work would seem to contend, old patriarchal deities are no longer satisfactory. What she has done is to profit from an established tradition to convey new values. Beyond mere formal changes, her *altares* replace the transcendental with the political. In them, the affirmation of feminist and Chicano experiences is more relevant than a pious communication with the celestial sphere. Such a secularization of home altars is evidence of their adaptability as well as their visual versatility.[19]

Chicano and Nuyorican artists are not alone in exploring home-altar aesthetics. Boston photographer Dana Salvo has exalted the tradition of Mexican home altars by uprooting them from their private context and presenting them as sites both of unorthodox beauty and of firsthand religious experience. Salvo transforms *altares* into objects of aesthetic contemplation: in elegant cibachrome prints, the colors, textures, and arrangements of *altares* stand out in all their splendor. For Salvo, an artist who has also focused on the recovery of lost or ruined textures (some of his other work consists of uncovering the debris and capturing the layers of time and decay in ruined mansions), the seduction of home altars is primarily visual. The absence of some contextualization to help decode home altars underlines their value as objects as well as their ultimate otherness: they represent a reality that speaks a different language. Still, even if the appreciation of *altares* is limited to an aesthetic discovery of their iconic attributes, this remains a relevant connection to a hitherto ignored cultural manifestation. Furthermore, the participatory process in which Salvo and the creators of the altars engaged when they rearranged the *altares* for the photos speaks for the reciprocal benefits of active cultural exchange.[20]

Finally, religious iconography is used as a format for modern experience in the work of Audrey Flack, who explores her own feelings through images of the Virgin Mary. For more than a decade, Flack has drawn from the Spanish Marian cult as a source of inspiration. Her choice of imagery is based on an identification with what she feels are analogous experiences of motherhood. Flack overdramatizes her Virgins, making them hyperreal by accentuating color, giving the paintings a glossy quality, and even adding glittery tears. It is this overdramatization that, together with the baroqueness of the imagery, makes her work "popular kitsch," a kitsch that takes itself seriously and is sentimental and Romantic. Flack distinguishes this kitsch from "art world kitsch," which in her opinion covers sentiment with humor. Emotional identification is the basis for her claim to a more valid relationship to religious imagery than that of other artists.[21] Flack's emotional affinity with the Virgins notwithstanding, her use of them is mainly functional and isolated from the Marian tradition as a whole. A syncretist, she takes elements from any religion that suits her needs, in an interchangeability that renders the specificity of religious traditions secondary.

Third-degree religious kitsch consists in a revalorization of Catholic iconography and the accentuation of those traits that make its aesthetics unique: figurativeness, dramatization, eclecticism, visual saturation—all those attributes for which kitsch was banned from the realm of art. In providing an aesthetic experience that transcends the object, kitsch is finally legitimized as art, an issue that has been of more concern to art critics than to kitsch artists. Consequently, it has been argued that the recirculation of kitsch is but a co-optation by the late avant-garde, a formal gesture of usurpation coming from its desperate attempt to remain alive.[22] There is little difference between the use of kitsch as a motif by the market and by avant-garde art, since the value of the icon lies for both in its exotic otherness, its ornamental ability to cover the empty landscape of postindustrial reality with a universe of images. Such pilfering of religious imagery is limited to reproduction, displacing and subordinating its social function but not altering the material in any significant way.

But what is happening in the third-degree revaluation of kitsch is more than the avant-garde's swan song. It is the collapse of the hierarchical distinction between the avant-garde and kitsch—and, by extension, between high and popular art—a collapsing of what modernity considered a polar opposition. According to this view, sustained principally by Clement Greenberg, the avant-garde revolution transferred the value of art from its sacred function (providing access to religious transcendence) to its innovative capabilities (leading to a newly discovered future via experimentation and disruption). Since kitsch is based on imitation and copy, countering novelty with fakeness and artificiality, it was consequently understood as the opposite of the avant-garde and considered reactionary and unartistic.[23]

Macarena Esperanza, 46 × 66 in. oil on canvas by Audrey Flack, 1971. Courtesy the
Hoffman Collection.

The current crisis of representation, however, implies not only disillusionment with progress, originality, and formal experimentation but also a reconsideration of all they excluded. It follows that copy, simulation, and quotation are raised to a new level of interest, representing a different experience of art and creativity. In postmodern culture, artifice, rather than commenting on reality, has become the most immediately accessible reality. Fakery and simulation were present in modernism as aesthetic means. They had a function, as in the reproduction of consumer society's alienation in Andy Warhol's work. In postmodernity, there is no space for such distances: fake and simulation are no longer distinguishable from quotidian life. The boundaries between reality and representation, themselves artificial, have been temporarily and perhaps permanently suspended.

Moreover, these boundaries are questioned not only by third-degree kitsch, but also by the current recirculation of kitsch. Anticipating this postmodern taste, Walter Benjamin wrote in a brief essay that kitsch is what remains after the world of things is extinct. Comparing it to a layer of dust that covers things and allows for a nostalgic recreation of reality, Benjamin believes kitsch—the banal—to be more accurate than immediate perception (thus favoring intertextuality over indexicality). For him, immediacy is just a notion of reality, and only the distance left by the loss of this immediacy permits a true apprehension of things. Therefore, he trusts dreams, rhythm, poetry, and distraction. Because of its repetitiveness—worn by habit and decorated by cheap sensory statements—kitsch is most suitable for this nostalgic resurrection, making for an easier and more pleasurable perception.[24] In discussing the Iconoclastes and their fury against the power of religious images, Baudrillard ascribes to simulacra a similar nostalgic function. Yet in his characteristic neutralization of signs, Baudrillard fails to assign them any discursive power.[25] Such empowerment is precisely the issue at stake in third-degree kitsch.

Besides imploding the boundaries of art and reality, the third degree carries out an active transformation of kitsch. Taking religious imagery both for its kitsch value and its signifying and iconic strength, it absorbs the icon in full and recycles it into new meanings. These meanings are related to personal spiritual experiences, recalling users' relationships to first-degree imagery, except that the first-degree images are part of a given cultural heritage and as such they are readily available and their usage is automatic. Third-degree kitsch, on the other hand, appropriates this tradition from "outside," searching for an imagery that will be adequate to its expressive needs. Its cannibalization of imagery, however, stands in sharp contrast to previous appropriations. In the early avant-garde, for instance in Picasso's use of African masks, the break with Western imagery had a symbolic function. Similarly, in surrealism and the release of the unconscious, exploring difference meant disrupting a cultural heritage perceived as limited and oppressive. Venerated for its ability to offer an experience in otherness, difference stood as the necessary counterpart of Western culture. Its function was to illuminate. Yet this assigned purposefulness tamed the perception of those cultures, ultimately erasing difference from the Western imaginary landscape.

In the work of the artists mentioned earlier, Catholic religious imagery provides access to a variety of intense emotions that seem otherwise culturally unattainable. In Salvo's photography the pleasure seems to come from the intimacy of the home altars, where family history is revered in a colorful clutter of figures and personal objects. This affectionate and ingenuous assortment stands in contrast to the photographic gaze through which it is perceived. For their viewers, the beauty of *altares* lies in their direct connection to reality, a connection that succeeds in stirring the capacity for amazement. A similar pleasure is found in Flack's virgins, whose melodramatic intensity becomes almost sublime, following the tradition of Catholic hagiography. Meanwhile, Mesa-Bains and other Chicano and Nuyorican artists are moving toward a radical transformation of tradition by imposing their own will on the material they work with, as in Mesa-Bains's use of *altares* to sanctify contemporary femininity.

This colonization of religious imagery, in which it is occupied by alien feelings and intentions, can be said to work in both directions. After all, the exotic, colonized imagery has now become part and parcel of the appropriator's imagination—it is part of the cannibal's system. Instead of appropriation annihilating what it absorbs, the absorbed invades the appropriating system and begins to constitute and transform it. The unsettling qualities of such cross-cultural integration are underscored by kitsch's syncretic tradition of mixture and pastiche. Since kitsch can readily exist in a state of upheaval and transformation, there is no eventual settlement of the absorbed. In the past, this reverse colonization has been minimized by adverse historical conditions. Yet the vast Latin American immigration to cosmopolitan urban centers in the past few decades is forcing a redefinition of traditional cultural boundaries, one that both shapes and is shaped by the circulation of images. If at one time exotic images were domesticated, they now seem to have lost their tameness to a newly found space: the one left by the exit of traditional referentiality. It isn't surprising then that third-degree kitsch in the United States is coming mainly from the East and West Coasts, since it is in these places that a new culture, deeply affected by Latinos, is being formed.

Religious imagery in third-degree kitsch surpasses the distance implied in second-degree kitsch. Instead of consuming arbitrarily, it constitutes a new sensibility whose main characteristic is the displacement of exchange by use. The consumption of images has been qualitatively altered: images are not chosen at random; they must convey a particular feeling, they must simulate emotion. Third-degree kitsch is the result of that search. Whether its potential destabilization will have a concrete social result before it is annihilated by a systematic assimilation that hurries to institutionalize it—making it into second-degree kitsch, for example—is debatable. Still, it is not a question of this assimilation seeping down into the depths of culture and carrying out some radical change there. After all, American culture is basically one of images, so that changes effected at the level of imagery cannot be underestimated. Since commodification is one of the main modes of integration in the United States, it can certainly be used as a vehicle of symbolic intervention. Third-degree kitsch therefore may be considered a meeting point between different cultures. It is where the iconography of a culture, instead of ceasing to exist, is transformed by absorbing new elements. Rather than of active or passive cultures, one can now speak of mutual appropriation. Even if an iconography is stolen it remains active, and the artists' work discussed here illustrates how this iconography can occupy the appropriator's imagination by providing a simulation of experiences the native culture has become unable to produce.

It can be said that each degree of religious imagery satisfies the desire for intensity in a different way: in the first degree through an osmotic process resulting from the collection and possession of objects still infused with use value; in the second degree by the consumption of commodified nostalgia; and in the third degree by cannibalizing both the first and second degrees and recycling them into a hybrid product that allows for a simulation of the lost experience. Even though they're produced at different moments, these three degrees cohabit the same contemporary space. Their synchronicity accentuates the erasure of cultural boundaries already present in third-degree kitsch, throwing together and mixing different types of production and perception. This reflects the situation of the urban cosmopolis, where myriad cultures live side by side, producing the postmodern pastiche. Such an anarchic condition destabilizes traditional hegemony, forcing it to negotiate with those cultural discourses it once could oppress. The ability of cultural imagery to travel and adapt itself to new requirements and desires can no longer be mourned as a loss of cultural specificity in the name of exhausted notions of personal or collective identities. Instead, it must be welcomed as a sign of opening to and enjoyment of all that traditional culture worked so hard at leaving out.

Four

Nature Morte

The wounded deer dragging its fainting limbs to some untrodden brake, there to gaze upon the arrow which had pierced it, and to die—was but a type of me.
Mary Wollstonecraft Shelley, 1817

Dr. Frankenstein weeps over the misfortune he has brought upon himself. His invention, the first manufactured creature—gentle at heart and desperately longing for affection, but a horrendous sight to behold—is shunned by everyone and has embarked on a bloody revenge that will annihilate his creator's entire family. Punished for the arrogance of artificially producing life, Frankenstein sins again by imaginarily dying an unnatural death—struck by an arrow—while depicting himself in the best tradition of still-life images: a wounded animal placidly representing death for the sake of human contemplation.[1]

The modern Prometheus's boldness consists of a repeated assault on one of nature's most elementary laws: metamorphosis, the ability of living things to change, to evolve into different forms until their final transformation into corpses.[2] High technology, the space age retro fashion, and a kitsch saturation of space all challenge natural metamorphosis in their respective ways. High technology and the space age retro fashion flatly deny the passing of time: the former by producing systems, such as cyborgs, apparently immune to natural deterioration; the latter by defying continuity in the replacement of time with space. A kitsch saturation of space ignores the natural laws of transition and renewal for the sake of a compulsive accumulation, exchanging diachronic sequence for the synchronic coexistence of different cultural layers.

Yet the temporal and spatial loss induced by high technology produced a melancholic sensibility that exceeds retro fashion's space age
personification and is scarcely compensated with iconographic baroqueness. Littered with high-tech trash and haunted by the abandoned remnants of a once-flamboyant modernity, modern cities, like
modern bodies, are attacked by a premature senility.[3] Obsessively fix-
ated on the body and the concrete reality it perceives as lost, this melancholia rebels in corpses, ruins, and both organic and technological
decay.

Melancholic Sensibility and the Scenification of Death

Postmodern culture, exhausted by ahistoric repetition, appears to have
psychasthenically resorted to spatial scenification to mourn its loss of
temporal dimension. Scatologically, melancholic sensibility offers an
alternative to the dizziness of hologramic fluidity in the rigor mortis of
dioramas, scenifying death in a way similar to Frankenstein's doubly removed literary example (first from himself as a human being, then as
the object of spectatorial gaze). After all, death stands for a fixation that
finds in the termination of life the beginning of an eternal existence.

Melancholic sensibility is the climactic moment of allegorical desire,
as discussed in chapter 2. Since the radical scenification sought by
allegory can only be attained in the separation of body and spirit in
death, corpses and ruins become its perfect emblems: shells empty of
meaning, sheer materiality. Opposed to the harmony of the symbol, allegory is anarchic; it counters the symbol's transcendental impulse
with an insistence on the irrevocable perishability of all things. Allegory
undermines the hierarchy granted by a symbolic aspiration to the spiritual with the banality of all human desires, facing them with death. In
its cult of fragmentation and decay, allegory stands as both a lamentation for the shattered dreams of modernity and a rebellion against the
premises on which they stood.

Whereas the symbol is imbued with a sense of totality and transcendence to which an alive, blossoming, nature is congenial, allegory
seeks to portray its perception of transitoriness and ultimate isolation
with a decaying, gray nature—the splintered and frozen remnants of a
wintry landscape. Dead leaves, stuffed animals, and rotting road kills
meet an urban/suburban landscape of industrial waste, deteriorated
machinery, and abandoned buildings in what could be considered a
subculture of junk and debris. In it, value stems from a beauty or gran-

diosity that is now in utter decay. The most insignificant remnant can evoke an imaginary world out of reach except for that fragment. Like a pentimento, the ruins of the city and the body surface from behind technological screens, producing a pastiche that simultaneously contains past, present, and future. More than a lamentation for what is lost, this melancholic sensibility is deeply imbedded in the intensity of the loss—not seeking to reconstitute what is gone, but to rejoice in its impossibility. The melancholic spirit lives contemporary culture as a splendorous and baroque memento mori, whose different layers must be uncovered like those of Pompeii.[4]

In his discussion on allegory, Benjamin distinguishes between the nostalgic experience, which produces corpses, and the melancholic one, which objectifies everything into a souvenir, "freezing" its death. Postmodernity combines the two; contemporary melancholia is capable of transforming nostalgic remains into souvenirs, as in the space age comeback and the current delight in ruins and decay. This combination is eerily illustrated in the use of stuffed piranhas and shrunken heads as tourist souvenirs, and in the emergence in the last few years of stores like New York City's Maxilla and Mandible and Old Harovian, which specialize in skulls, animal skeletons, animal fetuses, and similar realia. This obsession with death accounts for the current revitalization (so to speak) of still-life exhibits, with their corresponding lifeless bodies—a literal *nature morte*. Frozen in time, these corpses can only be understood spatially as volumes and textures, promptly qualifying for an aesthetic scenification such as the one provided by dioramas. As a mise-en-scène of life, dioramas follow the basic principle of both photography and memory: things must die in order to live on forever. A locus of conflict, death, and pain can be automatically aestheticized by the camera—or the photographic gaze in general—which makes trophies of even the most gruesome images. In a reversal of straight hunting, photographic "shooting" kills not the body but the life of things, leaving only the carcasses. Sempiternally freezing life into an object by making it into a still life, photographic and filmic shooting are reminiscent of turn-of-the-century camera safaris and their attempt to appropiate the foreign by capturing its images.[5]

Photographic contradictions therefore underline the issues where they surface. Hiroshi Sugimoto's black-and-white photographs of the American Museum of Natural History dioramas are a particularly interesting case in point. Sugimoto underlines the scenographic qualities of

WELCOME TO THE WORLD OF

OLD HAROVIAN

PURVEYORS OF ANTIQUES, CURIOSITIES AND NATURAL HISTORY SPECIMENS

Old Harovian was created to capture the spirit of the English Gentleman's home filled with the interesting and exciting pieces he had collected on his travels through out the world. "Old Harovian" is the name given to a graduate of Harrow, a 16th century English boarding school. Old Harovian was chosen because it represents some of Britain's oldest and most treasured traditions. Old Harovian has assembled rare and unique pieces from Europe, Asia and Africa for the discriminating collector. Everything at Old Harovian is authentic and available for sale; from the English partners desk to the human skeleton.

By combining strict scientific accuracy with an esthetic element, Old Harovian bridges the gap between science and art, helping people gain a better appreciation of the grandeur of our world. Old Harovian believes that saving specimens is as important as saving wildlife, for these may soon represent the only available study materials for many dwindling species.

SOME COMMONLY ASKED QUESTIONS:

Q: Who buys the natural history specimens?
A: Sculptors, painters, interior designers, photographers, propmasters, fashion designers, and people interested in Natural History.

Are the bones and specimens real?
Yes, everything at Old Harovian is authentic unless otherwise specified.

Where does Old Harovian get the skeletons and other natural history specimens?
Our natural history specimens are acquired from ranchers, trappers, game wardens and laboratories throughout the world.

OLD HAROVIAN, LTD.
175 West 4th Street
New York, N. Y. 10014
(212) 727-7208

OPEN DAILY 3PM TO 10PM , SATURDAY 12PM TO 10PM , SUNDAY 1PM TO 8PM

Flyer for Old Harovian, Ltd., 1988.

dioramas by exposing them as the still-life settings they are. The interpretation he proposes is generally clouded by the dioramas' pragmatic function: to be seen as "slices of life." This function relegates to a secondary status the aesthetic practices (photographic disposition of the elements, depth, "realistic" backdrops) and the ideologies (patriarchal organization, a survival-of-the-fittest selection of specimens) they reproduce.[6]

By reproducing dioramas in rigorous black and white, Sugimoto brings out the one-dimensional articulation of these arrangements, which is usually lost in the nuances of color, their sequential presentation, and a spectatorship that accepts them as realistic displays. Lacking the three-dimensionality that enhanced their verisimilitude, the dioramas exhibit in the photographs a newly found flatness that makes their stifling immobility more apparent than ever: specimens stare at the camera without a hint of life, forever stuck in the same position. Reduced in size and intentionally presented as artistic objects in Sugimoto's photos, the dioramas can come forth in the contradictory wonder of their artificiality.

As in Proust's childhood reminiscences and Kavafy's erotic longings, the thrust of life seems susceptible to appreciating this sensibility only through absence, a negative dialectic considered decadent for its indifference to movement, growth, and continuity. How lack of life and absence of color characterize *nature morte* is illustrated in two of the best-known episodes of decadent literature: Raymond Roussel's tableaux vivants (eight dead people in an enormous glass cage who through the injection of "resurrectine" come to life for a few seconds to act out the most important incident of their lives) and J. K. Huysmans's funerary dinner in honor of his lost virility, where everything, from the trees to the food, is black.[7]

The conjunction of image-saturation and *nature morte* is precisely the loss of the self in space or psychasthenia (compare chapter 1). Notably, it seems also to be the case in some epileptic seizures, in which the state of trance is accompanied by myriad images. One of the most remarkable cases is that of Gustave Flaubert, whose *Temptation of Saint Anthony* is loaded with baroque imagery representing the saint's temptations: food, riches, cities, a seductress. As Flaubert's play unfolds, St. Anthony sees the metamorphosis of one imagery into another, until he reaches ecstasy during his own transformation into these images, which he perceives as matter in a final collapse between the real and the imaginary:

> I'd like to have wings, a carapace, a rind, to breathe out
> smoke, wave my trunk, twist my body, divide myself up, to be

inside everything, to drift away with odors, develop as plants do, flow like water, vibrate like sound, gleam like light, to curl myself up into every shape, to penetrate each atom, to get down to the depth of matter—to be matter![8]

The apparent contradiction between a frenetic flow of images and the deadly immobility that produces it is resolved in allegory, where figurativity meets the palpability of death in the rendering of a concrete but transient universe. Aimée Rankin re-creates such a universe in her multimedia box series. Rankin's elaborate boxes are always cluttered with objects that contribute to the formation of a topical scenario, in an aesthetic reminiscent of the Catholic *altares* described in chapter 3. In Ecstasy, she addresses the issues of death and degeneration by incorporating such things as skulls, bones, and shark fetuses, presenting them through their reflections in mirrors. In Cruelty, allusions to transitoriness and theatricality are intensified as the box "comes to life" when the viewer dons a headset in which Bobby Darin can be heard singing "Mack the Knife." Rankin reproduces the connection between eroticism and death in its full contradiction. She forces the viewer to peep into the boxes and satiate visual desire in order to achieve a climactic moment of visual pleasure. At the same time, this process is made self-conscious through the size and artistic nature of the show, which serve as reminders of the exhibits' objectifying qualities and guarantee the viewer's aesthetic distance from them. This simultaneous fascination and distancing is intrinsic to *nature morte* exhibitions.[9]

Contra Natura: Physical Aberration as a Memento Mori

If death is life's final episode and annihilation underscores the contingencies of existence (all those things that, like time, were taken for granted), then the aberration of a natural order of things should also serve an allegorical function. This is probably why the cult of death is often accompanied by an almost perverse pleasure in physical deformities, freaks, accidents, and deviant behavior. While J. G. Ballard's fondness for mutilation and catalogs of failed suicides is consistent with his belief in the erotica of technology's speed and mechanical repetition,[10] other artists postulate that only a confrontation with the bizarre and grotesque enables the recovery of a sense of awe for death that is long lost to our culture. This is the explicit agenda of Gwen Akin and Allan Ludwig, who hunt for octopuses, pigeons, and pig snouts in local

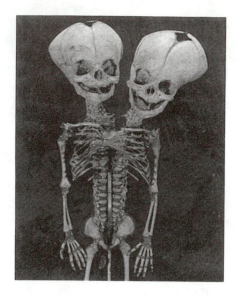

"Janus-Headed Skeleton," 5 × 4 in. platinum print. Copyright Gwen Akin and Allan Ludwig, 1986.

food markets, deer antlers in junk shops, and fetuses, deformed skeletons, and sliced human heads in medical museums—and then render them as platinum prints.

Claiming that our culture has systematically numbed a primal connection to death, Akin and Ludwig attempt to reestablish it in the contrast between the glittery texture of the prints and their grim subject. Inescapably confined to containers, print frames, and finally our own gaze, this dead matter reproduces the metaphoric fatefulness of photography while such an undesired immortality simultaneously speaks of its opposite, the fleetingness of all life. Adding to the complexity by way of simulation, the two-toned bareness of the prints makes them uncannily stale; they impress the viewer as dusty relics of other times.[11]

Inspiring both fascination and repulsion, these photographs refer back to the still-life tradition in which dead animals were laid side by side with, for example, kitchen utensils. A scene's verisimilitude was based on an exact rendering of its subject matter. This depiction, however, depended in turn on the use of a particular formalism deemed "realistic": the arranging of objects by size, color, and function as opposed to practical use.[12] In other words, the realism of the still-life genre always implied a subordination to the eye, to the act of being seen as an art object, rather than a fidelity to a reality that inevitably proved more chaotic. It is perhaps as a subversion and exposure of this genre that postmodern works like the ones analyzed here opt for an intensification of the dark and grotesque. In this way, they counter the repression of plurality and discordance effected by high technology, whose imposition of a binary system carries all the way from its selective criteria to its aesthetics (clean vs. dirty, shiny vs. opaque).[13]

The artificial, the scenographic, the physically aberrant, and the spectacular all meet in photographer Joel-Peter Witkin's extraordinary tableaux vivants. Often alluding to a cultural icon (Christ, Velázquez's *Meninas,* the myth of Leda), Witkin elaborates dramatic scenarios using deformed people (obese or anorexic, mutilated or dismembered) who are usually half or totally naked and either showing their genitalia or openly involved in a violent or painful sexual activity (fist sex, a duck biting a vulva, a man hanging by his testicles). For Witkin, as for Akin and Ludwig, violence is a constant reminder of the grandiosity of life.

The visual focus of Witkin's artistic work is in the painstaking artificiality of the mise-en-scène: backdrops are jaded and old, furniture and loose objects are arranged to look like props in a studio, people are in highly dramatic and uncomfortable poses and looking straight into the camera. This artificialness is furthered by the deliberate theatricality of the scenes, in which characters are often wearing some kind of mask, and draperies serve to emphasize and demarcate the scene as a stage. Not content with this sophisticated elaboration of elements, Witkin proceeds to chemically treat his negatives so the final outcome is as visually distorted as the scenes he depicts, blurry edges and scratched surfaces intensifying an awkwardness that denies all visual respite with its peculiar brand of *horror vacuii.*

Witkin's profound cynicism toward any notion of the natural (bodies, settings, acts, surfaces) consistently distorts preexisting images, disclaiming their uniqueness. What is more, in his intricate reelaboration of many of these icons, Witkin seems to be proposing culture as an infinite source of images that attract each other by the sharing of certain qualities. That is why his decadent scenarios abound in old furniture and torture machines, while his characters cover the spectrum of pain. His rendition of *Leda* (the mythological Spartan queen approached sexually by Zeus, who was impersonating a swan), for example, shows us a severely anorexic nude male holding a swan by the neck while looking up with an expression of total loss, face half-covered by a horizontal shadow. At her/his feet lie the shell of a gigantic egg and the bodies of two children, an allusion to Leda's own. Tainted so that spots of darkness and light randomly illuminate the print, this photo heightens the myth's sexual trespassing with the mixing of creature reproduction—children born from eggs. The intertextuality of images, rather than being an isolated phenomenon, becomes perfectly consistent with the moral and aesthetic breaking down of boundaries.[14]

One of Witkin's most ambitious pieces literally proposes how contemporary perception is constituted by images. His *Crucifix* depicts a Christ made up of thousands of photographs of a naked man printed on metal. His flesh, then, is the image of another's flesh, and it effectively carries the weight of the world. This peculiar exchange whereby images have come to take the place of the human body and psyche, that is, have moved beyond the perception of experience onto the body itself, was presented as a video installation in the 1989 Image-world exhibition at the Whitney Museum in New York City. The installation consisted of a darkened room with a small television set in which a woman was seen sleeping; the walls of the room were intermittently covered with her dreams—video footage of death and destruction accompanied by a "sensurround" effect. Viewers were in this way provided with a reversal of the usual presentation of images: these were not "real" (coming from the outside world) but rather unconscious images. Consequently, they scared most of an audience accustomed to treating (although not to experiencing) images as pertaining to an exterior realm susceptible to voluntary control.[15]

A Culturescape Made of Old Images, Junk, and Debris

Witkin's reelaboration of classic icons is symptomatic of melancholic desire, which, saturated by a culture of the new and its rapid obsolescence and obsessed with death, recycles or simulates old imagery incessantly. A good example from mass culture of the *nature morte* aesthetic is the current black-and-white trend in advertising, which attempts to bestow on its images a sense of oldness by rendering them as they would have been before color photography or color television. Many ads for clothes, drinks, and other items for consumption by a public under thirty are produced in two tones (black and white, sepia or gray), an occasional flash of bright color reminding us of their newness. This is true of a series of Calvin Klein clothing ads, infused with their own sex and death obsessions. Embodying the perfect urban fantasy, these ads present a phantasmagoric, postapocalyptic landscape of burnt trees, full of beautiful lost boys roaming around with their clothes half-torn by an unknown catastrophe. The sepia tones contribute to the feeling of desolation but at the same time allude to old photos, producing an uncanny conduit between past and future.

An urban landscape made of intertextual images has been correctly dubbed a "culturescape."[16] Constantly referring to a plethora of different times and cultures, with buildings from all epochs anachronistically aligned side by side, space becomes an imaginary territory where instead of a causal organization, a pastiche of seemingly random selections prevails. Unlike the depth and balanced distribution of elements that often govern landscapes (producing a certain "serenity")[17] or that once attempted a rational urban layout (the case of Brasília), contemporary culturescapes incorporate disparate elements and throw them together so as to underline their deliberate, or human-made, constitution. In this way, culturescapes also differ from the notion of organic growth, whereby cities extend and adapt to the requirements of their growing populations.

Thus, the recycling of old or "used" images takes place in a cityscape already saturated with the remains of different iconographies — the case of both high-tech debris and the ruins of modernity. Rather than a built-upon layer of antiquity that knows a complete process of growth and decay, the modern city soon becomes its own graveyard, housing the ghosts of its dreams shortly after coming to life. Based on the modern concept of replacement as opposed to a traditional notion of maintenance and perdurability, modern cities gallop well ahead of themselves in their ambitions, disregarding a supporting structure that soon collapses.[18] Defying a perception of the passing of time that would attribute decay and deterioration to old age, modern cities often display a mixed layering of times in which the carcasses of twenty- and thirty-year-old structures stand alongside buildings that have aged over centuries. As I suggested in chapter 2, the most striking illustration of such rapid decay is presented by Brasília, a city dead by the time its future arrived. Brasília's short life span must be measured against the paradoxical fact that the future it was planned for — the bright and efficient world of tomorrow so vehemently portrayed in the world's fairs — never took place.

It is in this sense that the postmodern melancholic sensibility is fostered not only by the evanescence of the organic but also by the quick turnover of high technology itself, which leaves behind it a wake of ob-

The postmodern culturescape. Ad from *Continental Profiles*, vol. 2, no. 5, May, 1989.

jects that have become obsolete overnight. In its race toward maximum efficiency, high technology produces artifacts whose only advantage is also their main handicap: they rely on a technological perfection that has aged by the time they are on the market. Generated incessantly, high-tech products are doomed to be out of competition in no time: they have to compete not only against myriad similar products but also against improved and updated versions of themselves (New York Telephone offered "obsolescence-free" services in 1988). Instantly depreciated, on sale the minute they're out, these products are also reproduced in clones that can boast their most seductive features at dramatically lower prices. Wide circulation of the already replaceable and obsolete provokes a market saturation that continually overflows, creating an urban landscape of high-tech trash. This phenomenon can be observed on Canal Street and in Times Square in Manhattan, in any major urban downtown, and to an even greater extent in high-tech production centers like Hong Kong and Tokyo, where the streets are paved with discounted computer software and hardware still expensive in other parts of the world.[19]

Accentuating the transitoriness of time so cherished by the melancholic spirit, this high-tech turnover also results in reproducing the displacement of time with space, by filling all the gaps left by the speed of production with the products themselves. Therefore, against a time progression so fast that it can no longer be sensed in the gradual aging of objects and consequently all but disappears from nonconceptual perception, we are left with a space full of practically unused objects. Age, for these objects, is not measured by the passing of time, but rather by the speed of production. Often made for a very short life span, these artifacts die without age marks, still shining new. Their deterioration is caused more by abandonment than by use: they are left to the decomposition occasioned by lack of maintenance and often relegated to the realm of trash. An extension of the industrial waste that surrounds and even inhabits most cosmopolitan cities, high-tech junk is a sad witness to the exhilarated production of our time.[20]

It is probably out of this intense disappointment in the future of technology and progress that a "new" version of junk art has surfaced, assisting in the constitution of a severely deteriorated culturescape. One of its best illustrations can be found in the Rivington Sculpture Garden in lower Manhattan, a conspicuous example of art made from debris collected in the streets. Slowly accumulating the classic items of dumps—old refrigerators, broken televisions, abandoned cars, rusty

Rivington Sculpture Garden, New York City, 1987.

market carts—community artists and inhabitants welded all these materials together, spray painting and fixing them to grates. The product is a bizarre interior landscape of waste, a garden of—and in—hell that brings to the fore how industrial and technological decay have replaced organic death in contemporary cities.[21]

What distinguishes postmodern junk art from its precursors—Picasso's and Schwitters's collages, Duchamp's objets trouvés, and more recently, the New York junk aesthetics of the 1950s—is precisely its ornamental quality. Current junk art is far from being concerned with the motivations that drove this tradition before (the subversion of surrealistic associations and the incorporation of everyday life into art), since these were primarily about redefining the boundaries or functions of art.[22] Instead, current junk art presents itself as either a continuation of the deteriorated urban landscape or as of strictly ornamental, and therefore commercial, value.

This fascination with urban decay is diversely manifested, from miniature three-dimensional landscapes made out of rust to glossy photographic shows of industrial rubble and abandonment to custom jewelry made of street debris. The acme of industrial wreckage frenzy is probably Survival Research Laboratories, a San Francisco performance

group whose act consists of the loud spectacle of machines destroy-
ing themselves and their surroundings. In an open-air performance
that usually entails the assistance of the local fire department, machines attack and demolish by remote control whatever they encoun-
ter, while spectators enjoy the closeness of physical danger in what
seems a nostalgic war exercise.[23]

Be it by way of reproducing a scenario of waste, providing trash
props for urban dwellers, or performing an act of industrial violence,
junk art can be said to fully participate in a melancholic sensibility that
clings to deadliness as the only coherent expression of postmodern
existence. Its recycling is peculiar in that it uses "fresh" debris instead
of old images, denying the nostalgia of times gone by in favor of the
melancholia for a death that is lived as a permanently present condition. Insofar as this aesthetics refuses to participate in an exclusively
artistic discussion, it promotes an explicitly political questioning of the
residual effects of industrialization, technology, and urban policies that
is often oriented toward a revalorization of the organic. Thus junk art is
reminiscent of those abandoned structures that have been slowly
taken over by roots and weeds—of the ruins of once-powerful empires
whose grandiosity has been humbled by the same nature they thought
to have mastered, yet whose sad beauty is magnified by this natural
invasion as by the most precious of human embroideries.[24]

Fake Scientific Exhibits and the Parody of Systematic Methodologies

Within the diverse *nature morte* substyles—diorama, still life, junk art—
one also finds an irreverent mixing and recycling that exposes the
genre's artificiality while furthering the perception of the world as a
dump of shattered illusions, old images, and obsolete discourses. The
ideological exposure of "deadly" discourses that until recently were
considered legitimate extends to the realm of scientific methodology,
whose unveiling is carried out using the same language on which it
rests. This is done by recreating old imagery in a slightly skewed manner, faking systematic methods like zoology or anthropology to an absurd degree, or dramatizing the artificiality of animal exhibits and doc-
umentaries. In this way, recycling and simulation succeed in casting a
critical commentary on the intention that produced those images and
exhibits while simultaneously retaining an allegorical pleasure often ignored by verbal deconstruction.

In *From the Pole to the Equator* (Yervant Gianikian and Angela Ricci Lucchi, 1986), the story of human physical conquest is told with turn-of-the-century footage. Rephotographed and hand tinted, what was originally meant as a documentary of exotic peoples and lands becomes through recycling an eerie object of contemplation. Substituting voice-over for music accentuates the bizarre familiarity of hunting and war scenes, making them all the more dramatic, as in the long and bloody hunt of two whales, in which the texture and rhythm of the ocean is intermittently interrupted by the frantic escape of the animals, counterposed in turn to the hunters' sneers. Accompanied by a minimalist score and constantly changing hues, the scenes appear almost unreal, fascinating us with the grotesque.[25]

A more humorous approach is found in Elayne Reicheck's installation The Revenge of the Cocoanuts: A Curiosity Room. In a room "tropicalized" by a small palm tree, dozens of coconuts scattered all over the floor, and simulated native weapons and paddles, she displays several blown-up photographs of the South Seas. Idyllic vistas such as a night view with palm trees and silver moon are partly covered by touristic postcards and photographs representing the Western view of the Other. Subversion takes place in the unnatural condensation of these images, which when placed together display the absurd panorama of colonial appropriation: white women dressed in pseudonative "panther" outfits, the extraordinary romanticization of a landscape shaped into vacationland, its people turned into curiosities. A particularly hilarious manifestation of colonial insensitivity and preposterousness is found in a photograph that shows several natives in front of a banner announcing a film. A caption voices the organizers' frustration over the natives' lack of interest in the movie, describing how they had to be cajoled into attending with presents of cigars and other bric-a-brac. Little did the natives know what was in store for them: the film was about cannibalism in the South Seas.

Reichek's work inverts traditional anthropology by making the conqueror's view itself into an objet trouvé. Instead of subjecting this view to a detailed conceptual analysis, she unmasks it by accentuating its object quality. She elaborates different aspects of the images: she blows up the colonial pictures, hand tints them, and sets them up in compositions. The artificiality of these images is intensified by the installation's simulated tropical scenario by way of the coconuts. Such inhabiting of the simulacra produces a strong secondhand sensory

Cannibals All, 22 × 42 in. oil photocollage by Elaine Reichek, 1988. Courtesy the artist and the Michael Klein Private Collection.

pleasure that complements an intellectual understanding of the images. This recreation of how others look at the world enhances the self-awareness of viewers, simultaneously stimulating and putting in perspective their own voyeurism.

Reichek further subverts anthropology by reproducing the task of a field researcher in what could be considered an urban hunt. Using the city as an exploration site, she shops around, gathering processed images and materials to work with. Based on associative collection and assemblage, her work illustrates the degree to which contemporary cities have become microcosms. Products and images from all over the world are available to consumers in many cities, making traveling and all its related activities unnecessary. Space and time are no longer defined by movement, but by exchange: they have become icons in the urban market, transforming urban experience into simulation. History and geography are just collections of postcards, maps, and souvenirs. The anthropology of our time is not made up of the objects of ancient peoples, but of their images: the ways in which they were seen by others. Substituting for all the other senses, the gaze shapes our perception so it registers the world as a huge diorama.[26]

A show that makes the hunting of images its explicit topic is Susan

Hiller's Dedicated to the Unknown Artists (also known as the Rough Sea project), a compilation of postcards whose common feature is the British coast. The postcards portray the coast from two main points of view: from the shore, showing a calm or rough sea—with or without ships—and from slightly off-shore angles that show the sea in relation to the cliffs, beaches, hotels, and small towns on the coast. Meticulously arranged in sets of thirty to thirty-six each, the postcards are systematically classified by their traits—photography, painting, monochrome, color, format, elements, caption, location, dedication, signature—in charts that are located next to the images.

Although they span a seventy-year period, these postcards appear to be depicting a single moment over and over again, an impression intensified by their proximity to one another. More than a representation, the image of the sea stands out as an icon, as if a certain ungraspable intensity had been forever captured in the postcards' simplicity. It is perhaps the eternal repetition of such a timeless moment that makes these images so fascinating. Instead of being effaced by their similarities, however, the postcards are individualized in the small details that differentiate them. This subjectivity, intensified by the "used" quality of the postcards (they have all been sent to someone, a fact that Hiller emphasizes in her categorization of the types of messages they contain), adds to the familiarity of an object as common as a postcard. Ultimately, this combination of "old wave" Romanticism and familiarity confers on the series a nostalgic quality often related to the act of collecting itself.

Rough Sea sets scientific analysis and sensory pleasure side by side, each casting its shadow on the other. The contrast between the imagery's complexity and the charts' arid methodology becomes a commentary on the science of classification. A former anthropologist, Hiller would seem to be declaring the irreducibility of images, their autonomy and perdurability. Furthermore, by turning the eye on methodology as an artistic object, she blurs the already hazy boundaries between science and art, undermining the claim of science to an objective reality.[27]

Scientific methodology is the subject of Fauna, a mock zoological installation that literally displays how compulsive accumulation of data can fake "the real thing." Claiming to have gained access to an early-twentieth-century German zoologist's archives, two Catalan artists set up Professor Peter Ameisenhaufen's finds. The installation includes photos, X rays, sound boxes, data cards in German, and stuffed specimens. Installed in carefully arranged vitrines along the walls, following the manner of a natural history museum, the exhibit also provides documentation on the German professor with pictures, letters, journals, and other mementos.

The creatures that this suspicious Dr. Ameisenhaufen so painstakingly recorded for science are without exception hybrids, sometimes even mixing the animal and vegetable kingdoms. This unusual pastiche imparts to these rare species both old and new attributes of confusion and deceit: the *Alopex stultus,* for instance, is a radioactive armored fox that in camouflage position passes for a shrub. These grotesquely assembled animals and their deceiving attributes undo the authority of a taxonomy that purports to have discovered and kept them in the name of human knowledge. Furthermore, the show's apparent severity gives way to a breaking of bounds that scientific discourses attempt to repress. The obsessive gathering of data is matched by the compulsion of recording it in detail on every possible register, something perhaps best illustrated in the tightly hand-written index cards, as well as in the imitation animal calls that sporadically travel through the room.[28]

The contemporary loss of the physical is mourned with an imagery of organic and urban decay. At first sight, the iconography of death, while consistent with the anxiety of loss and the fear of technology that have been discussed in previous chapters, would seem to be in direct opposition to space age and kitsch imagery, as full of movement, sentimentalism, color, and shine as they are. This apparent divergence, however, conceals more similarities than meet the eye. The method used in *nature morte* exhibits is based on both a pastiche of topics and textures and the recycling of images; consequently, its strategies—as in the reappropriation of kitsch and the retro fashion's space age personification—legitimize a self-conscious artificiality not only as an experience but also as a way of knowing.

Moreover, the transformation of the body into a scenario, its decontextualization from a historical process, and the replacement of an implicitly natural setting with one that is explicitly human made, all help establish this aesthetics' highly spectacular character, approximating the peculiar attributes of kitsch and space age iconographies. It is in the dramatization of the cultural tension between absence and overdetermination, realism and mise-en-scène, as well as in the ultimate distinction between permanence and transience, that the current reemergence of *nature morte* may be said to address explicitly the issues those other iconographies dealt with obliquely.

Furthermore, while anthropological discourses and their practices of looking and collecting are disclosed as perverse forms of appropriation, the images and methods of science and photography—paramount perpetrators of death in life—are confiscated to produce yet another scenario. In most of the work discussed in this chapter, "hunting" with the camera is stretched until it is turned around to become a magnificent exposition of the assumptions that initially generated it. The success of this unmasking is partly due to the spectator's familiarity with the images being depicted. The pleasure of recognition renders viewers more vulnerable, already paving the way for an unconventional reading of these images. Yet the decontextualization and reorganization of the original material produces a paradoxical distance from the same imagery that was so gleefully remembered. The conjunction of beauty and terror (abuse, torture, pain, death) bestows on these images the quality of radical experiences, making them almost unspeakable—perhaps the reason why they lack a significant verbal dimension.

Nature morte artists address the aestheticization of pain, the perdurability of death, and the constitution of the real through artifice. Instead of erasing what is disturbing, they repeat and simulate it to infinity. Rather than declaring a productive exhaustion, this fascination with preexisting images may be seen as a response to the physical disappearance promoted by high technology, wherein the palpable and figurative become, in consonance with allegorical desire, the most attractive qualities. Thus it is in the ruins of images that allegory and postmodern melancholic sensibility converge and exalt each other. Simulation declares absence through presence. It is a relic of what has ceased to exist. The return of *nature morte* is an allegory of the extinction of natural life.

Five

Tupinicópolis
The City of
Retrofuturistic Indians

Tupy, or not Tupy, that is the question.
Oswald de Andrade, 1928

If atrocity exhibitions and junk gardens are counterpoints to high tech, what about employing both electronics and its waste to construct a dancing retrofuturistic Indian city? Or confronting a still life of a dead turkey with its referent, both on identical kitchen tables, surrounded by vegetables and culinary implements? This kind of postindustrial-cul-ture-with-a-twist is typical of Third World urban centers, a sardonic re-minder that postindustrialism is not exclusively a metropolitan phenom-enon, but rather a condition particular to all those cultures, including postcolonial ones, where a fast, if irregular, industrialization has taken place.[1]

Latin America's own version of international culture tends toward a hyperrealism of uniquely parodic attributes. This "magical hyperreal-ism" often inverts the image of a colonized people humbly subservient to metropolitan discoveries into one of a cynical audience rolling over with laughter at what it perceives as the sterile nuances of cultures with very little sense of their own self-aggrandizement. Banalizing issues and objects by either making them literal or dramatizing their function is part of a long tradition of dealing with the unexpected changes and imposed or makeshift policies postcolonial countries are usually forced to face. Thus, contrary to Fredric Jameson's definition of contemporary pastiche (a blank collage), I will argue here that Latin America's current use of pastiche redeems some of the traditional qualities of parody, although with a layer of cynicism that was absent until now from its discourse.[2]

While the appropriation and transformation of elements that are felt as threatening is an old process, it is in these past years that it has reached the highest degree of complexity. This is mainly due to an unprecedented degree of reciprocal appropriation and mutual transformation whereby cultural change can no longer be said to be a matter of simple vertical imposition or ransacking, but is rather an intricate horizontal movement of exchange. Despite the inherent inequalities of sources and processes, this system of social recycling constitutes culture into a somewhat duty-free space in which, as in Hong Kong, Manaus (Brazil), and Isla de Margarita (Venezuela), all hierarchies are disrupted and humanistic justifications put aside in order to guarantee the free and prompt flow of cash for goods sold at wholesale value.[3]

For Latin American culture both at home and in the United States, this means at least three distinct types of cultural recycling that, as was seen in chapter 3 to be true of kitsch, cohabit in synchronized difference. The matter of direct, unmediated adaptation aside, the processes of cultural transformation that involve Latin America as an object, a subject, or both are: the Latinization of urban culture in the United States, the formation of hybrid cultures such as the Chicano and Nuyorican, and what I will call the pop recycling of U.S. icons of both Latin American and U.S. culture itself at the moment of postindustrialization.[4]

The Latinization of the United States

A survey of the first two types of acculturation will illustrate the peculiar characteristics of the third, especially the parodic attributes suggested above as the counterpart to contemporary melancholia. Latinization is a process whereby the United States' culture and daily practices become increasingly permeated by elements of Latin American culture imported by Spanish-speaking immigrants from Central and South America as well as the Caribbean. Inspired by an ever-growing population that is currently estimated at thirty million people, Latinization is obviously stronger in those areas where this immigration is more concentrated, for instance in New York City, Florida, Texas, and California.[5]

The several kinds of elements absorbed by U.S. mainstream culture differ in their degree of permeation. The most simple and elementary kind occurs with all foreign cultures that have come to the United

States and is part of the "melting pot" ideology: the commercial circulation of food and clothing, appreciated mostly for their exotic quality. Constantly reinforced as part of a distancing strategy that attempts to keep clear boundaries, the importance of this exoticism becomes most apparent in the distinction between the "American" and the "ethnic." These two widely misused terms ignore the physical frontiers of the United States and the social mélange on which its culture is based in order to promote a sense of original belonging and reinforce the isolation of incoming communities. Consequently, the consumption of exotica has very little influence on the culture within which it takes place.

Although it may seem that such isolation runs counter to the "melting pot" ideology, I would like to propose that in fact these two complement one another, for implicit in the notion of melting is the disappearance of peculiar traits, the erasure of those attributes that distinguish different cultures, making them potentially disruptive to an established system. In short, both as exotica and as alloy foreign cultures in the United States would seem to be doomed: in one case to perpetual marginality, in the other to acritical integration. Amidst the myriad struggles such limited options have triggered, it is interesting to note that even the term *melting pot* is beginning to age, giving way to more dynamic reformulations of the intricate cohabitation of cultures. An example of this is the recent official description of New York City as a "mosaic," a place where elements come together not to be dissolved, but to construct together a panorama.

This first type of acculturation process gains in complexity when mainstream culture begins to be infiltrated by fragmented and scattered elements of language, music, film, and iconography. Beyond Latino restaurants, outlets, and communities, Spanish has begun to invade advertising and colloquial speech. Started mainly as a marketing strategy to address the growing Spanish-speaking population, this trend has been picked up by cityspeak, where the regular use of words like *adiós, café* (coffee), and *nada,* among others, indicates a certain popular recognition of the confluence of Latino and mainstream cultures in the United States. In a city like New York, this phenomenon is not new: many words have been borrowed from other languages, particularly Yiddish, and adapted as colloquialisms. The case of Spanish, however, is a national phenomenon whose increasing diffusion is perceived as so culturally destabilizing that a purist reaction against it has been launched; movements like English Only have succeeded in imposing English as the legal official language in many states.

The effort to appropriate and reformulate Latino culture in an "American" version extends also to food, music, film, and iconography. I have already discussed the current fashion of Catholic religious iconography in chapter 3. As for food, the 1980s witnessed the proliferation of mixed restaurants that basically take one of two directions. The first could be called the high-tech rendition of "ethnic" foods: different staples are transformed into fast food, as in the case of Tex-Mex food, derived from Mexican cooking. The second is a less drastic transformation, and it consists in the blending of mainstream packaging strategies and administration with the typical food and decor of the country in question. The outcome is places like Bayamo and Benny's Burritos, which offer savory mixing and matching of the basic ingredients and staples of Chino-Latino (Chinese-Cuban) and Mexican cuisine respectively—in pink and green neon-lit restaurants. This atmospheric artificiality is meant to evoke the color and icon saturation with which most of Latin American and Caribbean culture is associated. Benny's Burritos does it metonymically through colors, Bayamo by creating an elaborate mise-en-scène of tropical motifs, namely an excess of coconut trees.[6]

Latin American musical instruments, rhythms, and popular songs are also being steadily adopted. In part, this has to do with the current "worldbeat" and "go global" music, eager to incorporate postcolonial rhythms. Movements like 1988's We Are the World and SOS-Racisme (France) have both capitalized on this music and thrust it to the limelight. American singer-composer David Byrne has adopted Caribbean and Brazilian melodies, and his recycled versions are barely distinguishable from the originals, adding to the prevailing pastiche of genres and nationalities.

Mainstream films that attempt to broach the question of Latino cultural integration approach it from a conventional point of view. Two recent ones are coincidentally about musicians: La Bamba (Luis Valdez, 1987), about 1950s rock singer Ritchie Valens, and Crossover Dreams (Leon Ichaso, 1985), about 1970s and 1980s salsa singer Rubén Blades. In these two rags-to-riches stories, the issue of maintaining Latino identity in relation to becoming a mainstream musician is diffused by the highly emotional narrative through which it is rendered. In the Valens film it becomes a question of being accepted by his girlfriend's father, and Valens's final and successful discovery of the intensity and marketability of his legacy's music happens totally by accident. In the other film, Blades's failed crossover is schematic and full of

Ad run in various issues of *Life* magazine, 1988.

dogma: blinded by money and success, he abandons his own community only to discover that he can't make it in the outside world, which
wanted him precisely for his ethnicity.

Rather than presenting the complexities of acculturation within the
social context in which they are negotiated—market competition, cultural prejudice, the distinct degrees of success and failure other musicians have achieved—both films decontextualize their main characters
in order to make them individual success (or failure) stories. In this

sense, the films accept a preexisting cultural narrative that measures the success of Latino integration into mainstream culture through outstanding achievement. By ignoring the more quotidian practices of integration of such a large community, these films reinforce the notion that marginalized groups have to excel in order to be accepted in the dominating culture.

These films stand in contrast to the more sophisticated treatment of second-generation immigrants in *Le Thé Au Harem* (Mehdi Charef, 1986) and *My Beautiful Laundrette* (Stephan Frears, 1985), in which the difficult integration of Arab and Pakistani youths in Paris and London respectively is shown as part of a broader context that includes their families, their peers, and their relationship to the labor market. Furthermore, in these two films the ambivalent and shifting feelings of the main characters toward their cultural identity is portrayed as a reformulation of the underlying conflict between modernity and tradition, a duality that has been shattered by the contemporary globalization of ethnic attributes.

Nostalgia as a Cultural Hindrance

It is within the paradigms of this duality that the second type of Latin American acculturation takes place: the emergence of hybrid cultures—Chicano, Nuyorican—that struggle to find a place within the United States while keeping intact a sense of belonging to quite a different tradition. Whereas Latinization implies the fragmentary incorporation of Latino elements into a fairly technologized discourse, as in the case of food, the formation of hybrid cultures tends to pull toward a more traditional setting, connected to the nostalgia for the homeland that characterizes first-generation immigrants. This nostalgia permeates the second generation in the form of highly ethnocentric values—or resistance to them, an adamant denial of the legacy—and a family-centered behavior that, coupled with inadequate housing, education, and job opportunities, promote the isolation they should fight against.

Perhaps one of the most extreme representations of Latino nostalgia may be found in the *casitas*, the small houses built on vacant lots by Puerto Ricans in the Bronx and Manhattan. Used as weekend clubs, *casitas* enact an altogether different space, that of memory. Resembling homeland architecture and colors, they install a piece of Puerto

One of New York's *casitas*. *Rincón Criollo*, photo copyright Martha Cooper and the Bronx Council on the Arts, 1988.

Rico right in the middle of New York City, enabling builders and neighbors to imaginarily transport themselves in time and space.[7]

On the other hand, the mixing of traditional and modern elements is not only fundamental to the survival of many artists but often the main issue of their work. Nuyoricans Pepón Osorio and Merián Soto, one a visual designer and the other a choreographer, work together to produce performances in which a visually exuberant scenario sets the scene for the questioning and reformulation of classic Latino values—machismo, women's roles—through mixed media (video, slides, etc.).[8] The little-known Latin Empire signed with Atlantic Records in 1989 for the first Spanglish hip hop single, "Puerto Rican and Proud"; one of its artists goes by the pseudonym Puerto Rock.[9] The complexities and implications of the constitution of Latino culture being beyond the scope of this chapter, it is important to note that it has been precisely this nostalgia that has kept the majority of Latino communities from developing the parodic distance characteristic of the third type of acculturation.

Latin American Postindustrial Pop

While Chicano and Nuyorican cultures are bent on protecting an identity continually threatened by both bias and market voracity, there is a tendency in Latin America and in some Latino groups in the United States to turn inside out the Latin American stereotypes produced by the United States and the postindustrial iconography thought to be primarily from the First World. This inversion succeeds in casting its own light over postindustrialism, throwing back the stereotypes reproduced in that iconography and capitalizing on the U.S. image of the postcolonial. Based on the strategies of anthropophagy and carnivalization, this recycling generates a pastiche that parodies the iconographic production of mainstream culture. Beyond a mere transitory laugh, however, this parody enables the formulation of a peculiar Latin American and Latino questioning of the issues of tradition, modernity, and postmodernity, and often a method that benefits economically from overturning them.[10]

Parody and role inversion are not only examples of how to resist colonial practices to the advantage of marginalized cultures, but also processes whose political and social implications indicate a more dynamic mode of acculturation than that of Latinization. This is probably due to the fact that Latinization takes place mainly through commodification, corporations having rapidly understood the market potential of both Latinos and Latin iconography. As opposed to this, the overturning strategies to be discussed here may be considered popular or spontaneous practices in which consumption is either secondary or fully displayed as consumption. The contrast between Latinization and Latin American postindustrial pop shows the versatility of a practice like appropriation.

An interesting illustration of the way postcolonial parody works can be found in an episode of what must be the most well-known South American popular festivity—Brazilian carnival. An old tradition involving both the local community, which prepares year round for the three-day extravaganza, and the international marketing of touristic goods, the carnival features as its main spectacle the parade of samba schools. Each school parades an *enredo,* or theme, with a magnificent display of outfits and dances called *fantasias* (fantasies). Made up of thousands of dancers and singers and several *carros alegóricos* (allegorical carriages) where the theme is recreated, each school dances its *enredo* for forty-five minutes along the Sambódromo, a long stadium that serves as an artificial avenue.

Built in 1985 in an official attempt to control the carnival and its profits, the Sambódromo is already an interesting metaphor of the dynamics between tradition and modernity on which the carnival dances and that is often the topic of its *enredos*. Before the Sambódromo was built, the carnival used to parade down one of Rio de Janeiro's main downtown avenues, accessible to all. The construction of the mile-long avenue that comes to life once a year automatically stratified the event, since tickets to enter the Sambódromo are beyond the means of many Brazilians; furthermore, the place is segmented by price, ensuring that the expensive private rooms, occupied by wealthy politicians or tourists, get the best view at the expense of literally obstructing the sight of the lower-priced benches. Yet perhaps the biggest paradox of this popular event can be found right outside the Sambódromo's walls, in the very poor neighborhood whose inhabitants have to watch on television the spectacle that develops only a few feet away from them.

The contradictions and exclusions of the process of modernity are often addressed by the carnival's *enredos*. One of the most brilliant of such thematic allegories left the issue of national identity—through which this conflict is usually articulated—aside, focusing instead on the mechanics and consequences of global urban reality. A retrofuturistic Indian metropolis, Tupinicópolis, was the second finalist in the 1987 competition for best "samba." Its theme described the Tupi Indians, happy inhabitants of an unbridled cosmopolis where, amid neon and trash, they ride supersonic Japanese motorcycles and play rock music, wearing the Tupi look: brightly colored sneakers, phosphorescent feathers, and blenders as headgear. Its *carros alegóricos* showed a high-tech urban scenario of mirrors, chrome, and plastic made in golden, silver, and electric colors and set up in expressionistic diagonals and spirals. In it were highways, skyscrapers, and neon signs: Shopping Center Boitatá, Tupinicopolitan Bank, Tupy Palace Hotel, and even a disco.

The humorous Tupinicopolitan aesthetic recycled Hollywood's postcolonial pop image, producing a sort of Carmen Miranda in 1987 Tokyo. It carnivalized both the perception of Latin America as "primitive" and the glamor and distance of high tech by putting them together: executive Tupi Indians skating around glittery cityscapes and consuming city life to the utmost. In so doing, this *enredo* brought forward two constitutive issues for Latin American and Latino culture. These issues help explain how the habit of simultaneously processing different cultures in Latin America anticipated postmodern pastiche and recycling to the point where it could be affirmed that Latin American culture, like most postcolonial or marginalized cultures, was in some ways post-modern before the First World, a pre-postmodernity, so to speak.[11]

The first of these issues is the ability to simultaneously handle multiple codes. The intersection of an alien perception of Latin America—whose supposed primitivity is ridiculed by turning its inhabitants into Indians—with the sophistication of a technological cityscape, however dramatized for the effects of parody, is an accurate representation of the cultural mix in which Latin America is developing. Accustomed to dealing with the arbitrary imposition of foreign products and practices, this culture has learned the tactics of selection and transformation to suit the foreign to its own idiosyncracy, thus developing popular integration mechanisms that are deliberately eclectic and flexible. Rather than reflecting a structural weakness, this infinite capacity for adaptation allows Latin American culture to select what is useful and discard what it deems unimportant.[12]

Having become a cultural trait, this acquired distance is practical in more ways than one: it enables a humorous perspective that often reveals the relativity of problems that are felt elsewhere as unique and overriding. The tropicalization that Tupinicópolis makes of high-tech culture, for instance, heightens the perception of its impersonality and consumptiveness without a trace of demagogy. The transitoriness and short life span of advanced technology capped this allegorical reflection on city life: the last *carro alegórico* was the Tupilurb, a pile of debris (abandoned cars, refrigerators, televisions) painted in gold. "Watch all that happiness, it's a smiling city," Tupinicopolitans sang of the volatile urban experience, "even trash is a luxury as long as it's real." If First World postindustrial countries assume the decadence of the modern belief in progress with either melancholy or a disillusionment that stylizes ruins—as punk does—"underdevelopment" carnavalizes this decadence. In a paradoxical anthropophagy, the postcolonial turns postindustrial culture into pop, making its emptiness kitsch.

The second issue that Tupinicópolis brings to the surface regarding the postmodern *avant la lettre* character of Latin American and Latino cultures has to do with its depiction of the self-referentiality of urban discourse. The growing visual and iconic qualities of contemporary perception have turned to the city as the foremost scenario, an endless source of ever-changing images. Intensified by the mirror reflections of corporate architecture, cities become a place to be seen rather than to be lived in. This spectacular self-consciousness (the consciousness of being a spectacle) is familiar to cultures that have been regarded "from above" by colonization. What can be more conscious than the allegorical parade of an imaginary city on an artificial avenue?

The familiarity of being observed possibly accounts for the qualitative distance of two exhibits dealing with the contemporary production of images. *A trama do gosto: Um outro olhar no cotidiano* (The Constitution of Taste: Another Look at Everyday Life) took place in 1987 in São Paulo and was part of that city's anniversary celebrations. Imageworld is a retrospective that opened at the Whitney Museum of American Art in New York City in fall 1989. In dealing with the same topic, these two exhibits followed two completely different paths. What is relevant here is the unconventionality and humor of the Brazilian exhibit in comparison to the traditional way the Whitney installed its show. Whereas the Whitney scarcely ventured (except in its precious few video installations) to upset the predictability of the museum walk, which was mainly linear and without opportunities for viewers to participate, the Brazilian exhibit portrayed the contemporary relationship to images in the format in which it is usually lived: the experience of being in a city.

Using an avenue, the Avenida Babalurbe, as an organizing figure, the particular shows of *A trama do gosto* were arranged so as to simulate the urban facades of stores, buildings, and parks that urbanites can appreciate while walking or riding in a car. From the daily exchange of postcards to the more educated pleasure of visiting art galleries, the show tracked down how looking is culturally constituted. One of the more striking presentations was *Arranha-Céu* (Skyscraper), where, protected by darkness and standing on a rooftop, the public could spy with binoculars through "windows," looking into video monitors that depicted domestic scenes. The cinematic fascination of anonymous spying was confirmed by this presentation's popularity: a long line climbed to the rooftop, and once they were there, viewers were glued to the binoculars. Not a guard was in sight in this exhibit, which was complete with sidewalk cafés and performances. Quite a contrast to the heavily guarded, hands-off show the Whitney presented as its own version of an image world, where seriousness, authority, and conventional spatial disposition were hardly dislocated by the scattered video installations.

Be it the transitoriness of technology or the visual constitution of contemporary sensibility, both Tupinicópolis and *A trama do gosto* clearly represent a humorous approach to contemporary experience. In this way, threatening situations and intricate issues become familiar to a mass audience that would otherwise remain marginalized from such sophisticated reflections on urban life. Consequently, these shows in-dicate not only the ability of Latin American culture to deal with the complexities of postindustrialism, but also how such humorous rever-sals can promote an awareness of these issues at a popular level and, in the final instance, show them within a broader context than their First World counterparts ever do.

Reinventing Roles in Postcolonial Culture

Extreme examples of the recycling of First World icons may be found in a sort of cultural transvestism whereby these icons, rather than being overturned, are driven to the limit. This kind of subversion acts not by a deconstructive dismantling but rather by saturation. The imposition of added layers of meaning (through the use of multiple codes and a self-conscious theatricality) transforms the icon into a baroque object whose weight distorts the effectivity of any one signification. Two exam-ples of such cultural transvestism may be found in the emergence of Superbarrio from the ruins of Mexico City's 1985 earthquake and in the casual adoption of punk gear by Chilean youth. The generalized es-tablishment of Latin American cultural transvestism can be appreci-ated in the intrinsic differences of these examples, since Superbarrio is a popular political phenomenon engaged in the social struggle to as-sist Mexico City's poor, whereas Chilean weekend punks are middle-class youths concerned mainly with fashion. Both, nevertheless, suc-ceed in reformulating the original roles and exposing the mechanisms that articulated them in the first place.

Superbarrio (Superslum) is a masked stranger who indirectly grew out of the governmental inefficiency in handling the 1985 earthquake that destroyed vast areas of Mexico City and who has come to repre-sent a growing popular mobilization that is dramatically rearticulating social policies in Latin America.[13] Superbarrio first appeared in 1987 to assist the newly formed Assembly of Barrios, an alliance of groups that pressed the government for rapid reconstruction of the city's devas-tated neighborhoods, in continuing its demands for housing reforms for the poor. Although anonymous behind his mask and outfit (red tights, gold cape, and shirt inscribed with the initials *SB*), Superbarrio has become a well-known national figure who is received in high gov-ernment offices and has extended his agenda to denouncing and fighting police corruption, pollution, and transportation problems—an

Film still Third World Newsreel from *Guerreros pacíficos*. Copyright Gonzalo Justiniano, 1985.

ambitious undertaking that, according to popular mythology, is really covered by four Superbarrios.

Rather than turning reality into a dream, which is what happens through mainstream media in the United States, Superbarrio, complete with a telephone hotline, a Barriomobile, and a Barrio Cave, inverted the formula: taking the superhero figure quite literally, he put it to work at the service of the needy. Whereas in the United States superheroes like Superman and Batman do little more than promote consumer goods and reinforce the good guys versus bad guys national ideology, in Mexico City popular appropriation of the superhero has replaced leisure consumption with the need for basic goods and a schematic narrative by a street struggle for the basic rights of the poor: "Our enemies are not imaginary, but real," says Superbarrio. Consistent with the popular power that enables his existence, Superbarrio keeps his mask on on the grounds that it allows collective identity.[14]

The case of Chilean punks is a role reversal of quite a different type. If Superbarrio politicizes the superhero figure, Chilean punks have managed to carry to the extreme the fashion industry's co-optation of punk. Initially, punk was a trend that sought to corporize the disillusionment of modernity and of the early 1970s hippie revolution in an aesthetics of bleakness and decay (in many ways like the one described in chapter 4, "*Nature Morte*"). The hard-core years of punk (roughly 1976 through the early 1980s) produced a dress code, music, and graphic language that used violence as a means of resistance to an apathetically established counterculture. This violence took the form of loud, dissonant music with accompanying melancholic or politically provocative lyrics; ragged black clothes that conveyed a state of physical deterioration; a lifestyle marked by an absence of past or future and therefore basically transient—without a permanent home or job, feeding off junk or stolen food; and an anarchist lack of belief in any kind of institution.[15]

In many ways, punk was the most conspicuous resistance to the cultural mainstream to come from within its native ranks. Mainly a white phenomenon, it grew out of the depressed London inner cities and was taken up soon after in New York City by middle-class youth, which makes Chilean weekend punks into an icon at second remove. Blank and defiant to the world and tied internally by a strong sense of peer alliance, punk soon began to emerge from the margins of cosmopolitan cities worldwide. Such a dramatic statement of style was rapidly co-opted by the fashion and music industries, which turned the aesthetics of decay into yet another mode of consumption. However obvious this may be in New York or London, it is in the Chilean making of punk into a pop icon of hipness that the contrast between its origins and its later versions can be best appreciated.

The "punk fashion" in Santiago, as portrayed in Gonzalo Justiniano's video *Guerreros pacíficos* (1985), must be distinguished from the punk underground that developed there, however small or contradictory it is. By contrast, Chilean weekend punks live a relatively established life and don punk outfits as party costumes. Delighted at the local commotion they cause, they wear elaborate makeup, dance rowdily, and gang up, but neither their aesthetics nor their attitude is connected to bleakness and violence. Instead, they are punk because *es la onda* (it's cool), and their detachment from the punk subculture as well as their highly iconic experience of it is perhaps best portrayed in their naive use of pins that say "Punk." By openly adopting punk as a fashion that in no way alters the rest of their life, Chilean weekend punks break the illusion that adopting a certain type of clothing can automatically grant a certain kind of experience, a founding illusion of U.S. advertising, which equates aesthetics with style and style with fashion, implying that in buying into the fashion you can acquire the aesthetics.

Unwittingly, Chilean weekend punks assist in exposing the mechanics of the fashion industry.

The iconic radicalism of Superbarrio and Chilean weekend punks is politically and artistically explored by San Diego's Border Art Workshop/Taller de Arte Fronterizo, a multidisciplinary group of Chicano, Mexican, and American artists who work to subvert the images of the border region that have been created by the media. Fascinated by crosscultural phenomena, the Taller de Arte Fronterizo is bent on understanding and reproducing hybrid cultures and uses the frontier as a metaphor for a place where different discourses intersect. To this effect, it recycles stereotypical iconography, in particular iconography that addresses the mixture of U.S. and Mexican clichés, as a politically powerful discourse, highlighting the potential strength of hybrid cultures over purist nationalistic exclusivities. The workshop explicitly addresses the brutal governmental tactics of U.S. border control in its installations and performances, many of which take place on site: on the border.

Among other interesting cases of cultural transvestism is the tongue-in-cheek acceptance of the primary icon for commercial uses. This is the case of innumerable tourist industries that simulate traditions and situations to fit tourists' expectations as a means of survival. As opposed to an organized tourism that creates a reality of its own, these industries are on the fringe of that market and benefit from it but are the product of the survival skills and the ingenuity of a people accustomed to having to meet others' demands and finally cashing in on those demands. Thus, the Hollywood transformation of Carmen Miranda into an icon of luscious tropicality finds its counterpoint in, say, a trio of astute Mexicans who, under the guise of being "authentic Aztec dancers," make a living from the gullibility of tourists in Niagara Falls.[16] These "authentics" manage to capitalize on the belief that Latin America is a "primitive" culture by practicing a sophisticated cultural transvestism that allows them to become what they are expected to be without the schizophrenia it usually engenders in the First World. Their ability to benefit from the icons of themselves by putting them on stage for a profit goes a lot farther in undoing racist clichés than most theoretical deconstructions. By appropriating such icons and manipulating them at will, popular culture demonstrates its unequaled mastery in recycling, the game only a high-culture postmodernity was supposed to play.[17]

ON WHICH SIDE OF THE BORDER IS THE AVANT-GARDE?

Photomontage by Guillermo Gómez-Peña, founding member of the Border Art Workshop/Taller de Arte Fronterizo. *On Which Side of the Border Is the Avant-Garde?* 1988.

It is in this third type of acculturation, the one that banks on its hybrid character to participate in and overturn the paradigms produced by the First World, that the most exciting cultural proposals of the moment can be found. Leaving behind postindustrial melancholia and identity nostalgia, and to the side market globalization of ethnicity, the humorous overturning of mass media images, like the artistic exposure of scientific disciplines I discussed at the end of chapter 4, works exclusively within the iconic realm to proclaim it a flexible language that may be bent, twisted, and turned to satisfy far more needs than the ones that produced those icons in the first place. Trained by a long history of intertwining codes and spectacular roles, postcolonial cultures show in this reversal how the world can also be a scenario for their own directorial and spectatorial delight.

Epilogue

Bodies are becoming like cities, their temporal coordinates transformed into spatial ones. In a poetic condensation, history has been
replaced by geography, stories by maps, memories by scenarios. We
no longer perceive ourselves as continuity but as location, or rather
dislocation in the urban/suburban cosmos. Past and future have been
exchanged for icons: photos, postcards, and films cover their loss. A
surplus of information attempts to control this evanescence of time by
reducing it to a compulsive chronology. Process and change are now
explained by cybernetic transformation, making it more and more difficult to distinguish between our organic and our technological selves.
It is no longer possible to be rooted in history. Instead, we are connected to the topography of computer screens and video monitors.
These give us the language and images that we require to reach others
and see ourselves.

Almost a relic, the body is exercised and sanitized to glorification. It
is the last refuge of identity. Like the vanishing city, the body remains as
the only concrete proof of existence. Yet, scattered and fragmented under the weight of technology, body and city can't be recovered by
means other than those that displace them: they must be recorded or
registered anew. Video replaces the personal diary. Made up of images, urban culture is like a hall of mirrors, its reflections reproduced to
infinity. Confronted with their own technological images, the city and

the body become ruins. Even technology is attacked by an obsolescence that renders it old instantly. We are faced with a transitory landscape, where new ruins continually pile up on each other. It is amid
these ruins that we look for ourselves.

Notes

Prologue

1. See Walter Benjamin, "Allegory and Trauerspiel," *The Origin of German Tragic Drama,* trans. John Osborne (London: New Left Books, 1977): 159-235; "Central Park," *New German Critique* 34 (Winter 1985): 32-58; *Charles Baudelaire: A Lyric Poet in the Era of High Capitalism,* trans. Harry Zohn (London: Verso, 1983); "The Work of Art in the Age of Mechanical Reproduction," *Illuminations,* trans. Harry Zohn (London: Jonathan Cape, 1970): 219-53. For a thoroughly researched description of the evolution of Benjamin's thinking and work see Susan Buck-Morss, *The Dialectics of Seeing: Walter Benjamin and the Arcades Project* (Cambridge, Mass.: MIT Press, 1989).

2. Gilles Deleuze and Félix Guattari, *Rhizome (Introduction)* (Paris: Editions de Minuit, 1976). Semiotics studies culture as a system of signs, analyzing how those signs constitute meaning. See Roland Barthes, *Mythologies* (Paris: Editions du Seuil, 1957) and "Semiology and the Urban," in M. Gottdiener and Alexandros Ph. Lagopoulos, eds., *The City and the Sign: An Introduction to Urban Semiotics* (New York: Columbia University Press, 1986): 87-98; Umberto Eco, *Il Segno* (Milan: ISEDI, 1973) and *Tratado de Semiotica General* (Barcelona: Lumen, 1977); Kaja Silverman, *The Subject of Semiotics* (New York: Oxford University Press, 1983).

3. Michel de Certeau, *The Practice of Everyday Life* (Berkeley: University of California Press, 1984).

4. By popular culture I mean the multiple ways in which vast numbers of people relate to urban life and events—a definition that includes mass culture but excludes folk art.

5. Angela McRobbie, "Postmodernism and Popular Culture," in Lisa Appignanesi, ed., *Postmodernism,* ICA Documents, vol. 4 (London: Free Association Books, 1986): 165-79. Tania Modleski, "Femininity as Mas(s)querade: A Feminist Approach to Mass Culture," in Colin MacCabe, ed., *High Theory/Low Culture: Analysing Popular Television and Film* (New York: St. Martin's Press, 1986): 37-53; "The Terror of Pleasure: The Con-

temporary Horror Film and Postmodern Theory," in Modleski, ed., *Studies in Entertainment: Critical Approaches to Mass Culture* (Bloomington: Indiana University Press, 1986): 155-67.

6. Donna Haraway, "A Manifesto for Cyborgs: Science, Technology, and Socialist Feminism in the 1980s," in her *Primate Visions: Gender, Race, and Nature in the World of Modern Science* (New York: Routledge, 1989).

7. Néstor García-Canclini, *Culturas híbridas: Estrategias para entrar y salir de la modernidad* (Mexico City: Grijalbo, forthcoming).

8. Walter Benjamin, "The Work of Art in the Age of Mechanical Reproduction."

9. Jean-François Lyotard, *The Postmodern Condition: A Report on Knowledge,* trans. Geoff Bennington and Brian Massumi (Minneapolis: University of Minnesota Press, 1984); Jürgen Habermas, "Modernity—An Incomplete Project," trans. Seyla Ben-Habib, in Hal Foster, ed., *The Anti-Aesthetic: Essays on Postmodern Culture* (Port Townsend, Wash.: Bay Press, 1983): 3-15. For a critical survey on the postmodern debate see Andreas Huyssen, "Mapping the Postmodern," *New German Critique* 33 (Fall 1984): 5-52. Thanks to Andreas Huyssen for his support during the writing of this book.

10. Michel de Certeau, *Practice of Everyday Life,* 96.

11. See Chantal Mouffe's lucid discussion on this topic in her "Radical Democracy: Modern or Postmodern?" in Andrew Ross, ed., *Universal Abandon? The Politics of Postmodernism* (Minneapolis: University of Minnesota Press, 1988): 31-45.

12. Gerald E. Stearn, ed., *McLuhan: Hot and Cool: A Critical Symposium with a Rebuttal by Marshall McLuhan* (New York: Dial Press, 1967).

13. Umberto Eco, *Apocalipticos e integrados ante la cultura de masas,* trans. Andres Boglar (Barcelona: Lumen, 1968).

14. Jean Baudrillard, "The Ecstasy of Communication," trans. John Johnston, in Foster, *The Anti-Aesthetic,* 126-34, and *Simulations,* trans. Paul Foss, Paul Patton, and John Johnston (New York: Semiotext[e], 1983).

15. Chantal Mouffe, "Radical Democracy," in Andrew Ross, ed., *Universal Abandon?*, 35.

16. Quoted in Andrew Ross, ed., *Universal Abandon?*, xii.

17. Fredric Jameson, "Postmodernism; or, the Cultural Logic of Late Capitalism," *New Left Review* 146 (July-August 1984): 53-92.

18. It does seem overzealous, however, to attribute to feminism the primacy of difference, as Andreas Huyssen and Craig Owens do when they claim feminism plays a founding role in postmodernism. For if difference is a practice of inclusion that integrates discordant elements, it is as constitutive of feminism as of the other discourses mentioned here that exercise a similar politics; it is in feminism, however, that difference is best articulated theoretically. See Craig Owens, "The Discourse of Others: Feminists and Postmodernism," in Foster, *The Anti-Aesthetic,* 57-82; Andreas Huyssen, "Mass Culture as Woman: Modernism's Other," in Modleski, *Studies in Entertainment,* 188-208; and Laura Kipnis, "Feminism: The Political Conscience of Postmodernism?" in Ross, *Universal Abandon?* 149-166.

19. I am following Mikhail Bakhtin's distinction between a monological textuality with a univocal and centered meaning, and a dialogical textuality that is pluralistic and intertextual. See Michael Holquist, ed., *The Dialogic Imagination: Four Essays by M. M. Bakhtin* (Austin: University of Texas Press, 1981).

20. I am privileging a Lacanian psychoanalytic reading of the structuring of the social. For a brilliant reading of Lacan, see Silverman, *The Subject of Semiotics.*

21. Frederic Jameson, "Postmodernism," in *New Left Review* (July-August 1984): 61-2.

22. See also Joel Fineman, "The Structure of Allegorical Desire," *October* 12 (1980): 46-66.

One   Reach Out and Touch Someone

1. Roger Caillois, "Mimicry and Legendary Psychasthenia," trans. John Shepley, *October* 31 (Winter 1984): 16-32. The full name, as Caillois refers to it, is "legendary psychasthenia." I have dropped the term *legendary* since its connotations might prove confusing. The appropriateness of psychasthenia as a trope is confirmed by the current circulation of Caillois's article; see Severo Sarduy, *La simulación* (Caracas: Monte Avila Editores, 1982).

2. See Paul Virilio, *L'espace critique* (Paris: Christian Bourgois, 1984), and *Estética de la desaparición* (Barcelona: Anagrama, 1988). On the hologram see David Bohm, *Wholeness and the Implicate Order* (London: Routledge & Kegan Paul, 1980).

3. Lewis Carroll, *Alice's Adventures in Wonderland* (Norwalk, Conn.: Heritage Press, 1969).

4. This is the Lacanian mirror stage in identity constitution. My discussion of the imaginary and symbolic is based on Lacanian theory. See Jacques Lacan, *Ecrits* (Paris: Seuil, 1966). For an excellent discussion of these aspects of Lacanian theory see Kaja Silverman, *The Subject of Semiotics* (New York: Oxford University Press, 1983).

5. Judith Williamson, *Consuming Passions: The Dynamics of Popular Culture* (London and New York: Boyars, 1986).

6. See Jean-François Lyotard, *The Postmodern Condition: A Report on Knowledge,* trans. Geoff Bennington and Brian Massumi (Minneapolis: University of Minnesota Press, 1984), and Fredric Jameson, "Postmodernism; or, the Cultural Logic of Late Capitalism," *New Left Review* 146 (July-August 1984): 53-92. For a panorama of the postmodern debate, see Andreas Huyssen, "Mapping the Postmodern," *New German Critique* 33 (Fall 1984): 5-52.

7. This is the concept of simulation advanced by Jean Baudrillard, *Simulations,* trans. Paul Foss et al. (New York: Semiotext[e], 1983); see also Michel Makarius, "La strategie de la catastrophe," *Traverses* 10 (1978): 115-24. A good case in point is the Vietnam War, whose construction as a media spectacle has been the matter of many studies and films. See Stanley Kubrick's *Full Metal Jacket* (1987) and the special issue "American Representations of Vietnam," *Cultural Critique* 3 (Spring 1986).

8. For an illuminating discussion of the power struggle behind the real/simulacra polemic, see Gilles Deleuze, "Plato and the Simulacrum," trans. Rosalind Krauss, *October* 27 (Winter 1983): 45-56.

9. Susan G. Sawyer, "Out of Control: The Fear and Loathing of Obsessive Compulsive Disorder," *New York Post,* May 17, 1989; Judith L. Rapoport, M.D., *Obsessive Compulsive Disease in Children and Adolescents* (Washington, D.C.: American Psychiatric Press, 1989).

10. See J. G. Ballard's science fiction, particularly his novel *Crash!* (New York: Vintage Books, 1985) and its introduction, as well as his interviews in *Re/Search* 8/9 (1984).

11. In the morning of August 25, 1986, in the Central Park area directly behind the Metropolitan Museum, Robert Chambers, 20, strangled Jennifer Levin, 18, to death. The prosecution claimed that he tried to steal money from her to support his cocaine habit and killed her after she discovered and confronted him. He alleged in his defense that they had had rough sex and the pain had led him to kill her. Both her corpse and his body indicated a fierce fight had taken place between them.

12. "New York City's Preppie-Murder Trial," *A Current Affair,* May 16, 17, 1988. On Chambers's confession tape see Emily Praeger, "Half-True Confessions," *Village Voice,* April 5, 1988; on Fox's "New York City's Preppie-Murder Case," see Emily Praeger, "Prime Time Porno," *Village Voice,* May 31, 1988: 51, and Amy Taubin, "Art Imitates Death," *Village Voice,* May 31, 1988: 51.

13. Thanks to Anne McClintock for suggesting this connection, as well as for the conversations we had on this and other issues relevant to this chapter. Cinematic voyeurism as a form of perversion was lucidly documented in *Rape* (Yoko Ono, 1968), in which a woman is assaulted by the obsessive chase of a cameraman filming her every movement for several hours. See J. Hoberman, "Making a Spectacle," *Village Voice,* March 14, 1989: 57.

14. For shrewd coverage of the trial, see C. Carr's "Who's on Trial," *Village Voice,* October 27, 1987: 19, and "Jack Litman's Little Murders," *Village Voice,* March 8, 1988: 14. On hyperreality see Mario Perniola, "Icones, Visions, Simulacres," trans. Michel Makarius, in *Traverses* 10 (1978): 39-48, and Umberto Eco, *Travels in Hyperreality: Essays,* trans. William Weaver (San Diego: Harcourt Brace Jovanovich, 1986).

15. See, for example, "America's Most Wanted." For a discussion of these programs see Amy Taubin, "Cop Shop," *Village Voice,* June 27, 1989: 53-4. A reversal of these programs happened recently in *The Thin Blue Line* (Errol Morris, 1988). During the film's reconstruction of the murder of a police officer, it became apparent that the wrong man had been convicted, opening the way for a public demand to appeal his case. This exchange between reality and fiction demonstrates once again the precariousness of their boundaries. Things have become even more complicated since the man was released and sued the filmmaker over the film rights.

16. About the social construction of illnesses as metaphors see Susan Sontag, *AIDS and Its Metaphors* (New York: Farrar, Straus & Giroux, 1988) and *Illness as Metaphor* (New York: Farrar, Straus & Giroux, 1978). For the ways of sexual paranoia see Arthur and Marilouise Kroker, *Body Invaders: Panic Sex in America* (New York: St. Martin's Press, 1987). For an interesting account of male schizophrenia and paranoia regarding female sexuality, and the politics of clean versus dirty in bodies and spaces, watch *Dead Ringers* (David Cronenberg, 1988); thanks to María Negroni for this suggestion and for her enthusiastic support of this chapter.

17. Mary Wollstonecraft Shelley, *Frankenstein; or, The Modern Prometheus* (New York: Collier Books, 1978).

18. See Gabriele Schwab, "Cyborgs: Postmodern Phantasms of Body and Mind," in the issue "On Technology (Cybernetics, Ecology, and the Postmodern Imagination)," *Discourse* 9 (Spring-Summer 1987): 64-84.

19. On the simulacrum, see Deleuze, "Plato and the Simulacrum." For identity formation and the oedipal elements in *Blade Runner,* see Giuliana Bruno, "Ramble City: Postmodernism and *Blade Runner,*" *October* 41 (Summer 1987): 61-74.

20. Philip K. Dick, *Blade Runner (Do Androids Dream of Electric Sheep)* (New York: Ballantine, 1982).

21. This is one of Lyotard's main proposals in *The Postmodern Condition.*

22. CBS Late News, New York City, July 21, 1988. The episode about "Circuit Breaker" mentioned here appeared in Marvel Comics, "Monstercon from Mars," *The Transformers* 1, no. 45 (October 1988).

23. Michel Foucault, *Discipline and Punish: The Birth of the Prison* (New York: Pantheon, 1977); Allan Sekula, "The Body and the Archive," *October* (Winter 1986): 3-64; Jacques-Alain Miller, "Jeremy Bentham's Panoptic Device," *October* 41 (Summer 1987): 3-29.

24. Gary Marx, "I'll Be Watching You," *Surveillance: An Exhibition of Video, Photography, Installations* (Los Angeles: LACE, 1987). In the past five years, the number of singles who check out their lovers through private investigators has quadrupled: see Frank Bruni, "Suspicious Singles Tail New Lovers," *New York Post,* June 18, 1989. There have been several incidents of private mail being opened at the post office. The most publicized have had to do with supposed child pornography. In one case, a woman's artistic portraits of her nude children almost cost her custody. In another, a mail-order reply for pornographic videos featuring children led to the busting of an alleged child pornography operation.

25. Eric Alliez and Michel Feher, "Notes on the Sophisticated City," *Zone* 1-2 (n.d.): 40-55. In a strange reversal of observer and observed, billboards might soon be recording passersby as part of a new strategy of market targeting in advertisement; see Bernice Kanner, "The Great Outdoors," *New York,* September 4, 1989: 19-22.

26. Thanks to Julia Scher for this suggestion, which she is currently exploring in her mixed-media installations on surveillance. Scher's work has greatly influenced my awareness of surveillance practices.

27. Donna Haraway, "A Manifesto for Cyborgs: Science, Technology, and Socialist Feminism in the 1980's," *Socialist Review* 80 (1985): 65-107.

28. See Jan Zimmerman, *Once upon the Future: A Woman's Guide to Tomorrow's Technology* (New York: Pandora, 1986).

Two   Lost in Space

1. For the articulation of this duality in a postmodern Latin America, see Néstor García-Canclini, *Culturas híbridas: Estrategias para entrar y salir de la modernidad* (Mexico City: Grijalbo, forthcoming). In this chapter, image means a simple visual representation as opposed to icon, which implies a cultural load: a specific set of images conforms an iconography. Therefore, both images and icons function as signs, although with different degrees of indexicality. For the different degrees of signs see Roland Barthes, *Mythologies* (Paris: Editions du Seuil, 1957). Thanks to Jean Franco for her suggestions regarding the organization of this chapter.

2. For an analysis of the circulation of decontextualized architectural signs see Robert Venturi, Denise Scott Brown, and Steven Izenour, *Learning from Las Vegas: The Forgotten Symbolism of Architectural Form* (Cambridge, Mass.: MIT Press, 1985). Artificial ruins have an interesting antecedent in the eighteenth century; see Phillipe Junod, "Future in the Past," *Oppositions* 26 (Spring 1984): 42-63.

3. My discussion of allegory is inspired by Walter Benjamin, particularly "Allegory and Trauerspiel," in his *The Origin of German Tragic Drama,* trans. John Osborne (London: New Left Books, 1977): 159-235, and "Central Park," in *New German Critique* 34 (Winter 1985): 32-58. See also Craig Owens, "The Allegorical Impulse: Toward a Theory of Postmodernism," in Brian Wallis, ed., *Art After Modernism: Rethinking Representation* (New York: New Museum of Contemporary Art, 1984): 203-35; Susan Buck-Morss, "Historical Nature: Ruin," in *The Dialectics of Seeing: Walter Benjamin and the Arcades Project* (Cambridge, Mass.: MIT Press, 1989): 159-201.

4. As proposed by Joel Fineman in "The Structure of Allegorical Desire" *October* 12 (1980): 46-66.

5. I disagree with Paul Smith's argument that allegory's nostalgia for truth is equivalent to the symbolic legitimization of truth. It is this nostalgic distance that enables allegorical deconstruction. See Paul Smith, "The Will to Allegory in Postmodernism," *Dalhousie Review,* Spring 1982: 105-22.

6. On the hierarchical disruption caused by simulacra see Gilles Deleuze, "Plato and the Simulacrum," trans. Rosalind Krauss, *October* 27 (Winter 1983): 45-56.

7. On the melancholic's fixation with death, see Sigmund Freud, "Mourning and Melancholia" (1917), translation supervised by Joan Riviere, *Collected Papers,* Vol. 4 (New York: Basic Books, 1959): 152-70.

8. The substitution of intensity for feeling is among the salient features of a techno-logized culture. Already anticipated by Benjamin (see "The Work of Art in the Age of Mechanical Reproduction," *Illuminations,* trans. Harry Zohn [London: Jonathan Cape, 1970]: 219-53) it has been discussed as "the waning of affect" by Fredric Jameson in his "Postmodernism; or, the Cultural Logic of Late Capitalism," *New Left Review* 146 (July-August 1984): 53-92 and is one of J. G. Ballard's main issues (see his interviews in *Re/Search* 8/9 [1984]: 6-52). On the use of catastrophic narratives, see Michel Makarius, "La strategie de la catastrophe," *Traverses* 10 (1978): 115-24.

9. For a discussion on utopia and a desired otherness see Fredric Jameson, "Progress Versus Utopia; or, Can We Imagine the Future?," in Brian Wallis, ed., *Art After Modernism,* 239-52. Jameson's reading of science fiction as a mere narrative projection of the present ignores the allegorical dimension of that genre, which I will argue accounts for its popularity and is also its most distinguishing feature.

10. See Fred Davis, *Yearning for Yesterday: A Sociology of Nostalgia* (New York: Free Press, 1979) and Randall Rothenberg, "The Past is Now the Latest Craze," *New York Times,* November 29, 1989.

11. For a good account of space age aesthetics—complete with illustrations—see Joseph J. Corn and Brian Horrigan, *Yesterday's Tomorrows* (New York: Summit, 1984).

12. Space age architecture and motifs grow largely out of architect Le Corbusier's International Style—a style that dates back to the 1920s and greatly influenced North and South American architecture, among others.

13. For the New York World's Fairs, see *Remembering the Future: The New York World's Fair from 1939 to 1964* (New York: Queens Museum, 1989). For a critical reading of the New York World's Fairs as corporate promotion, see Ed Ball, "Degraded Utopias," in *All's Fair,* a supplement celebrating the anniversary of these fairs, *Village Voice,* Fall 1989: 3-8.

14. It is commonly agreed that Romanticism's anthropocentricity marked the beginning of modernity.

15. For the rapid aging of new cities see Claude Lévi-Strauss, "São Paulo," in his *Tristes Tropiques,* trans. John Russell (New York: Atheneum, 1972): 100-108.

16. For the concept of subcultures, see Dick Hebdige, *Subcultures: The Meaning of Style* (London: Methuen, 1979).

17. For an analysis of yuppiedom, see Barbara Ehrenreich, "The Yuppie Strategy," in her *Fear of Falling: The Inner Life of the Middle Class* (New York: HarperCollins, 1990): 196-243.

18. For camouflage and the gay body see Severo Sarduy, *La Simulación* (Caracas: Monte Avila, 1982).

19. Quoted from a Film Forum program. Beginning in 1987, the New York Film Forum has held a popular summer festival of fantasy and science fiction, showing the films mentioned here and many others to sold-out audiences.

20. Benjamin distinguishes between two types of experience according to their relationship to time: *Erfahrung* is intrinsically related to the past, living out of memories (nostalgia), and seeing the remnants of that past as corpses (carrying the mark of time); *Erlebnis* (lived experience) is basically present, living the past as fragmented remembrances (melancholia) and seeing its remnants as objects free of time, souvenirs. See "Central Park" in *New German Critique.* This distinction is fundamental to understanding

contemporary vicarious pleasure. Whereas nostalgia sees the past as past (however golden), melancholia refuses to accept the death of the past, extending it temporally into the present.

Three   Holy Kitschen: Collecting Religious Junk from the Street

1. For a description of contemporary hyperreality see Umberto Eco, *Travels in Hyperreality: Essays,* trans. William Weaver (San Diego: Harcourt Brace Jonvanovich, 1986) and Jean Baudrillard, *Simulations,* trans. Paul Foss, Paul Patton, and John Johnston (New York: Semiotext[e], 1983).

2. I would like to thank the following people for allowing me to repeatedly photograph in their stores: Sam and Silvia at Sasson Bazaar, 108 W. Fourteenth Street; Maurice and David at Esco Discount Store, 138 W. Fourteenth Street; and Jamal at Sharon Bazaar, 112 W. Fourteenth Street. Fourteenth Street's internationality can be fully appreciated in these people's polyglotism: most of them speak four or five languages, including English, Spanish, Hebrew, Arabic, and French.

3. Little Rickie is located at 49 ½ First Avenue (at the corner of Third Street). Thanks to Phillip Retzky for letting me photograph in the store. The prices quoted are from 1987, when this chapter was written.

4. Available at Hero, 143 Eighth Avenue, and Amalgamated, 19 Christopher Street.

5. Much has been written about the video pope. For his 1984 visit to Puerto Rico see Edgardo Rodríguez Julia, "Llegó el Obispo de Roma," in *Una noche con Iris Chacón* (n.p.: Editorial Antillana, 1986): 7-52. For his 1986 visit to France see the wonderfully illustrated "Pape Show" issue of the French daily *Liberation,* October 4 and 5, 1986: 1-7.

6. Amalia Mesa-Bains, Grotto of the Virgins, Intar Latin American Gallery, New York City, 1987; Dana Salvo, Mary (group show), Althea Viafora Gallery, New York City, 1987; Audrey Flack, Saints and Other Angels: The Religious Paintings of Audrey Flack, Cooper Union, New York City, 1986.

7. Fredric Jameson, "Postmodernism; or, the Cultural Logic of Late Capitalism," in *New Left Review* 146 (July-August 1984): 53-92.

8. "In a vase of Kitsch flowers there is a formal defect, but in a Kitsch Sacred Heart the defect is theological," says Karl Pawek in "Il Kitsch Cristiano," in Gillo Dorfles, *Il Kitsch* (Milan: Gabriele Mazzotta Editore, 1969): 143-50. For another view of religious kitsch see Richard Egenter, *The Desecration of Christ* (Chicago: Franciscan Herald Press, 1967). For kitsch in general see Hermann Broch, "Kitsch e arte di tendenza" and "Note sul problema del Kitsch," trans. Saverio Vertone, in Dorfles, *Il Kitsch,* 49-76, and "Art and Its Non-Style at the End of the Nineteenth Century" and "The Tower of Babel," in *Hugo Von Hoffmannsthal and His Time: The European Imagination 1860-1920,* trans. and ed. Michael P. Steinberg (Chicago: University of Chicago Press, 1984): 33-81 and 143-83. Gillo Dorfles's book is a compilation of essays on kitsch, several of which will be mentioned throughout this chapter. See also Matei Calinescu, "Kitsch," in *Five Faces of Modernity* (Durham, N.C.: Duke University Press, 1987): 223-62; Haroldo de Campos, "Vanguarda e Kitsch," in *A Arte no horizonte do provavel* (São Paulo: Editorial Perspectiva, 1969): 193-201; Umberto Eco, "Estilística del Kitsch" and "Kitsch y cultura de masas," in *Apocalípticos e integrados ante la cultura de masas* (Barcelona: Lumen, 1968): 81-92; Clement Greenberg, "Avant-Garde and Kitsch," in *Art and Culture* (Boston: Beacon Press, 1961): 3-21; Abraham Moles, *Le Kitsch, L'Art de Bonheur* (Paris: Maison Mame, 1971). Aimée Rankin's "The Parameters of Precious," *Art in America* (September 1985): 110-17, was brought to my attention after the completion of this chapter; some of her arguments about the recycling of kitsch coincide with my understanding of it as pertaining to a vicarious sensibility.

9. Hermann Broch, *Hugo Von Hoffmannsthal,* 170.

10. The concept of cultural cannibalism was advanced in a different context by Oswald de Andrade, *Do Pau-Brasil a Antropofagia e as Utopias,* Obras Completas, vol. 6 (Rio de Janeiro: Civilizaçao Brasileira-Mec, 1970).

11. For some art theoreticians, this is a "primitive" confusion between referent and representation. See Aleksa Celebonovic, "Nota sul Kitsch tradizionale," in Dorfles, *Il Kitsch,* 280-89.

12. Décio Pignatari, "Kitsch e repertório," in *Informaçao. Linguagem. Comunicaçao* (São Paulo: Perspectiva, 1968): 113-17.

13. Gillo Dorfles, *Il Kitsch,* and Clement Greenberg, "Avant-Garde and Kitsch."

14. Hermann Broch spoke of the "kitsch-man" in Gillo Dorfles, *Il Kitsch,* 49.

15. This term was first used by Abraham Moles, *Le Kitsch,* 161-86.

16. For camp sensibility see Susan Sontag, "Notes on Camp," in *Against Interpretation and Other Essays* (New York: Octagon, 1982): 275-92.

17. See Walter Benjamin, "The Work of Art in the Age of Mechanical Reproduction," in *Illuminations,* trans. Harry Zohn (London: Jonathan Cape, 1970): 219-53.

18. Ceremony of Memory, Museum of Contemporary Hispanic Art (MOCHA), New York City, 1989. Ironically, this is happening at a time when Hispanics are said to be turning away from Catholicism. See "Switch by Hispanic Catholics Changes Face of U.S. Religion," *New York Times,* May 14, 1989.

19. For a more extensive account of Mesa-Bains's work and of *altares* in general see Tomás Ybarra Frausto's essay "Sanctums of the Spirit—The Altares of Amalia Mesa-Bains," published in the catalog for this show.

20. In his artist's statement for the Pastorale de Navidad show (Nielsen Gallery, Boston, 1987), Salvo describes this exchange: "The Polaroid process quickly dispelled any apprehension or superstition that arose, and the instant image generated an enormous amount of enthusiasm. Soon a crowd of villagers would be about the camera and house. They were moved that their creations were being photographed, and they treasured the Polaroids, displaying the image as part of the altarpiece. . . . Once everyone was accustomed to the photograph they would oftentimes arrange the interiors to better fit the frame. Or, this would encourage others to add small treasures to an altar as it would be seen minutes later in a Polaroid image."

21. Personal interview with Lowery S. Sims, published in the catalog for Flack's Cooper Union show.

22. Gerardo Mosquera, "Bad Taste in Good Form," *Social Text* 15 (Fall 1986): 54-64. For another view on Cuban artistic kitsch see Lucy R. Lippard, "Made in the U.S.A.: Art from Cuba," *Art in America* (April 1986): 27-35. For kitsch in the United States see J. Hoberman, "What's Stranger Than Paradise?" in "Americanarama," *Village Voice Film Special,* June 30, 1987: 3-8.

23. This is Greenberg's main proposal. See also Miriam Gusevich, "Purity and Transgression: Reflections on the Architectural Avantgarde's Rejection of Kitsch," Working Paper no. 4, published by the Center for Twentieth Century Studies of the University of Wisconsin-Milwaukee, Fall 1986.

24. Walter Benjamin, "Traumkitsch," in *Angelus Novus, Ausgewählte Schriften,* vol. 2 (Frankfurt am Main: Suhrkamp, 1966): 158-60.

25. Jean Baudrillard, *Simulations,* 7-9.

Four   *Nature Morte*

1. Mary Wollstonecraft Shelley, *Frankenstein; or, The Modern Prometheus* (New York: Collier, 1978). For a recent discussion on still-life aesthetics see Norman Bryson,

"Chardin and the Text of Still Life," *Critical Inquiry* 15 (Winter 1989): 227-52, as well as the texts in *Natura Naturata (An Argument for Still Life)* (New York: Josh Baer Gallery, 1989).

2. For a discussion of the connections between metamorphoses and death see Michel Foucault, "The Metamorphosis and the Labyrinth," in his *Death and the Labyrinth: The World of Raymond Roussel* (Garden City, N.Y.: Doubleday, 1986): 75-96.

3. For the rapid aging of new cities see Claude Lévi-Strauss, "São Paulo," in his *Tristes Tropiques,* trans. John Russell (New York: Atheneum, 1972): 100-108. In modern bodies, AIDS causes an ostensible decomposition (loss of hair, wrinkling of skin, muscular deficiencies) that recalls the signs of old age.

4. On the melancholic's fixation with death see Sigmund Freud, "Mourning and Melancholia" (1917), translation supervised by Joan Riviere, in *Collected Papers,* vol. 4 (New York: Basic Books, 1959): 152-70.

5. For an example of camera safaris see William Nesbitt, *How to Hunt with the Camera* (New York: Dutton, 1926). Trying to trap a certain reality by freezing it in time and making it more concrete through the print is the subject of Allan Sekula's study of criminal records; see his "The Body and the Archive," *October* (Winter 1986): 3-64.

6. Hiroshi Sugimoto's dioramas were exhibited in June 1988 at the Sonnabend Gallery. His fascination for theatricality extends to the rest of his photographic work; he has a whole series on old theater interiors. The Sonnabend exhibit was accompanied by a photocopied review by John Yau, "Hiroshi Sugimoto: No Such Thing as Time." On dioramas, see Donna Haraway, "Teddy Bear Patriarchy: Taxidermy in the Garden of Eden, New York City, 1908-1936," in her *Primate Visions: Gender, Race, and Nature in the World of Modern Science* (New York: Routledge, 1989).

7. Marcel Proust, *Au Recherche du Temps Perdu* (Paris: Gallimard, 1919-1923); Konstantin Kavafis, *The Complete Poems of Cavafy,* trans. Rae Dalven (New York: Harcourt Brace Jovanovich, 1976); Raymond Roussel, *Locus Solus* (New York: Riverrun Press, 1983); J. K. Huysmans, *Contra Natura* (Barcelona: Tusquets, 1980).

8. This epileptic characteristic is explained in Kitty Mrosovsky's introduction to Gustave Flaubert, *The Temptation of Saint Antony* (New York: Cornell University Press, 1980): 6, 232.

9. Three of Aimée Rankin's magic boxes Ecstasy series were exhibited during summer 1989 in the Whitney Museum of American Art at Philip Morris.

10. See his interview with Andrea Juno and V. Vale in *Re/Search* 8/9, 6-35. This whole issue is dedicated to Ballard and, in keeping with this aesthetic, mostly illustrated with Ana Barrado's photos of abandoned swimming pools and houses and barren landscapes. *Re/Search* has dedicated issues to torture, to body ornamentation with tattoos and other physical marks, and to freaks.

11. Akin and Ludwig were exhibited in the Farideh Cadot Gallery, New York City, in summer 1988. Their work is consistent with the current public outcry about animal torture.

12. On the exchange between art-effect and reality-effect in photography see Rosalind Krauss, "A Note on Photography and the Simulacral," *October* 31 (Winter 1984): 49-68; see also Bryson, "Chardin and the Text of Still Life." His discussion on the deadly objectification of still life is particularly interesting.

13. Artist Laurie Anderson has explored the implications of the binary system in her multimedia performances.

14. See the catalog for the retrospective of Witkin's work at the Spanish Centro de Arte Reina Sofía in 1988. (*Joel-Peter Witkin* [Madrid: Ministerio de Cultura, 1988].) Witkins also published an anthology of photos of medical aberrations.

15. Bill Viola, *The Sleep of Reason,* 1988

16. The term was coined by Braco Dimitrievic in *Natura Naturata.*

17. I am thinking of the Hudson River School's denial of industrialization in its depiction of an idyllic landscape.

18. Claude Lévi-Strauss, *Tristes Tropiques,* trans. John Russell (New York: Atheneum, 1972).

19. Christopher Johnston, "Electro-Excess," *Village Voice,* electronics supplement, May 17, 1988: 10-11.

20. Hazardous-waste processing was estimated as a five-billion-dollar industry in 1989. Associated Press, "Glowing Future in Toxic Waste," *New York Post,* March 14, 1989.

21. The Rivington School was located at Forsyth and Rivington until it was forced by gentrification to relocate one block up to Stanton Street.

22. See Roni Feinstein's essay in the exhibit catalog *The "Junk Aesthetic" Assemblage of the 1950s and Early 1960s* (New York: Whitney Museum of American Art, 1989).

23. See Guy Trebay, "Machine Dreams," *Village Voice,* May 24, 1988: 19-20.

24. On the struggle between the organic and junk in New York City see Sarah Ferguson's "The War of the Gardens," *Village Voice,* June 13, 1989. Frank Stella has worked with rusty grates and soda can cutouts, most recently a series of "Indian birds." Less well known, Luca Pizzorno is creating a mythology out of rusty material, which he sees as natural insofar as he regards decay as a natural process of death. It is worth noting how at the peak of high tech there is an increasing interest in "natural" and organically grown food, countering the artificiality and instantaneity of fast food. Natural and fast foods reach an intermediate point in the trendy "salad bars."

25. *From the Pole to the Equator* was screened at Film Forum 1 in April 1988.

26. Elaine Reichek's Revenge of the Cocoanuts was exhibited at the Bleecker Gallery, New York City, in summer 1988.

27. Rough Sea was shown at the Pat Hearn Gallery, New York City, in summer 1988.

28. Fauna was exhibited at the Museum of Modern Art, New York City, in summer 1988.

Five   Tupinicopolis: The City of Retrofuturistic Indians

1. On how postindustrialism affects Latin American culture see Néstor García-Canclini, *Culturas híbridas: Estrategias para entrar y salir de la modernidad* (Mexico City: Grijalbo, forthcoming).

2. See Fredric Jameson, "Postmodernism; or, The Cultural Logic of Late Capitalism," *New Left Review* 146 (July-August 1984): 53-92. An interesting comparative account of how this process of banalizing or parodying U.S. cultural production is done in Brazilian film may be found in Joao Luiz Vieira and Robert Stam, "Parody and Marginality: The Case of Brazilian Cinema," *Framework* 29 (1985): 20-49. Thanks to George Yúdice for this reference as well as for his suggestions and support during the writing of this chapter.

3. This image of postmodernity corresponds to the notion of wholesale changes in capital formation and their adaptation and reformulation by social representations as discussed in Paul Smith, "Visiting the Banana Republic," in Andrew Ross, ed., *Universal Abandon? The Politics of Postmodernism* (Minneapolis: University of Minnesota Press, 1988): 128-48. However lucid this article may be, Smith, like Jameson in "Postmodernism," doesn't seem to take into account postcolonial strategies of resistance. For a good overview of the main issues of the postmodernist polemic, see Andreas Huyssen, "Mapping the Postmodern," *New German Critique* 33 (Fall 1984): 5-52.

4. The question of unmediated adaptation has been discussed by theorists of imperialism and neocolonization. Néstor García-Canclini, in *Culturas hibridas,* goes to great lengths to discuss the degree and implications of such adaptation, showing that it is seldom as mechanical as it has been made out to be. He proposes that the irregularities of both the nationalism and modernizing processes in Latin America are made apparent by postmodernism's flattening of distinctions.

5. On the reaction to Latinization see Thomas B. Morgan, "The Latinization of America," *Esquire,* May 1983: 47-56.

6. Paul Smith in "Visiting the Banana Republic," in Andrew Ross, ed., *Universal Abandon?,* shows how the Banana Republic stores effect a similar process to neutralize and legitimize colonial discourse.

7. On the *casitas* see Joseph Sciorra, "I Feel Like I'm in My Country," *TDR* 34 (Winter 1990): 156-68. Also see Dinitia Smith, "Secret Lives of New York," *New York,* December 11, 1989: 41-2.

8. On Pepón Osorio and Merlán Soto, see Joan Acocella, "Loisaida Story," *7 Days,* November 9, 1988, and my "El difícil arte de montar escenarios," *Más,* Winter 1989: 71.

9. Guy Trebay, "Hip Hop in Spanglish," *Village Voice,* April 11, 1989: 19-20. For more on Latinization see Juan Flores and George Yúdice, "Living Borders/Buscando América: Languages of Latino Self-Formation," *Social Text* 24 (1990): 57-84.

10. See Joao Luiz Vieira and Robert Stam, "Parody and Marginality," which follows the notion of carnivalization put forth by Mikhail Backtin. See also Afranio M. Catani and Jose I. de Melo Souza, *A chanchada no cinema brasileiro* (São Paulo: Brasiliense, 1983); Celso F. Favaretto, *Tropicalia: Alegoria, Alegria* (São Paulo: Kairos, 1979); Benedito Nunes, *Oswald Canibal* (São Paulo: Perspectiva, 1979); Haroldo de Campos, "Da razïo antropofágica: a Europa sob o signo da devoraçao," in *Obras Completas de Oswald de Andrade,* vol. 2 (Rio de Janeiro: Civilizaçïo Brasileira, 1971).

11. This idea has been suggested by, among others, Guillermo Gómez-Peña in "A New Artistic Continent," *High Performance,* 1986.

12. On Latin American selective adaptation and transformation in literature see Angel Rama, "Los procesos de transculturación en la narrativa Latinoamericana," *La novela en América Latina: Panoramas 1920-1980* (Colombia: Procultura, 1982): 203-34.

13. For the recent popular movements in Latin America see "The Homeless Organize," *NACLA* 4 (November-December 1989), a special issue on this topic. Thanks to Jean Franco for this reference and for her suggestions on the writing of this chapter.

14. Larry Rohter, "The Poor Man's Superman, Scourge of Landlords," *New York Times,* August 15, 1988.

15. Dick Hebdige, *Subculture: The Meaning of Style* (London and New York: Methuen, 1979).

16. As told by Guillermo Gómez-Peña, one of the founding members of the Taller de Arte Fronterizo.

17. A similar ridiculization of and profit from tourists' expectations is depicted in *Cannibal Tours* (Dennis O'Rourke, 1988).

Index

Abortion, politics of, 17, 18
Advertising: image of technology in, 12; recycling of images in, 5-6; referentiality in, 64-65
African mask imagery in Western painting, 53
AIDS: image of the body and, 9-10; and surveillance strategies, 18
Akin, Gwen, 61-63
Alice's Adventures in Wonderland, 3-4
Alien, 31
Allegory: in Brazilian carnival, 83-85; and postmodern sensibility, xx-xxi, 41-42, 57-58, 61-64, 69, 74; and space-age retro, 19-24, 34-35; and symbol, 21-24, 35, 57-58. *See also* Benjamin, Walter; Smith, Paul
Altars, home, 38-39, 42, 47-49, 53, 61
American Museum of Natural History, 58-60
Anderson, Laurie, 103n.13
Anthropology. *See* Science, parody of
Anxiety: and experience, 23-24; and technology, 29-31, 34, 64. *See also* Technology; Woman as threat
Architecture: postmodern urban, 64-66, 84-85; and psychasthenia, 2; space-age, 24-29. *See also* Culturescape

Art: aesthetic enjoyment and vicariousness, 40; Catholic iconography in, 38; early avant-garde vs. postmodern, 53; vs. kitsch, 50; violence in, 63-64. *See also* Altars; Flack, Audrey; Junk art; Kahlo, Frida; Kitsch; Mesa-Bains, Amalia; Rankin, Aimée; Picasso, Pablo; Still life
AT&T. *See* Telecommunications
Attack of the 50-foot Woman, 31

Back to the Future, 30
Ballard, J. G., 7, 15, 61, 97n.10
Baudelaire, Charles, xii
Baudrillard, Jean, xv, xvi, 52. *See also* Simulation
Benjamin, Walter: on allegory, xx-xxi, 58, 99n.5; anticipating the postmodern gaze, xii; on kitsch, 52; on loss of the aura, xiii, xvii; on two types of experience, 58, 100n.20
Binary system and high technology, 63
Blade Runner, 11-12, 15
Blades, Rubén, 78
Body: and fashion, 32; fragmentation of, 7-18, 92-93; as organic, 11-14, 17-18; and technology in science fiction, 24,

29-30. *See also* AIDS; Cyborgs; Disease; Replicants; Woman as threat
Border Art Workshop, 89, 90
Brasília, 28, 65
Brazil, 82-85. *See also* Carnival; Manaus; Rio de Janeiro; São Paulo; Tupinicópolis
Brazil, 28
Breakdancing, 16-17
Bronx, 80-81

California, 76
Canal Street, 67
Capitalism, xvi-xviii, 104n.3; and the ethnic as commodity, 19
Caracas, xvi, 25
Carnival, 82-83. *See also* Tupinicópolis
Carroll, Lewis, 3-4
Casitas, 80-81
Castle, William, 33
Cat Women of the Moon, 33
Chambers, Robert, 8-10, 13
Charef, Mehdi, 80
Chicano: artists, 53; home altar tradition, 47-49; as hybrid culture in U.S., 81-82. *See also* Mesa-Bains, Amalia
Circuit Breaker. *See* Comic books
City: and body as fragmented, 92-93; decay of modern, 65-69; and self-consciousness, 84-85; Third World, 25, 75. *See also* Architecture; Brasília; Caracas; Hong Kong; Manaus; Montreal; New York; Paris; Rio de Janeiro; Santiago; São Paulo; Washington, D.C.
Comic books, 12, 14. *See also* Superbarrio
Coppola, Francis Ford, 30
Corporations, 26-28. *See also* Architecture; Telecommunications
Crash! 7, 97n.7
Cronenberg, David, 29
Crossover Dreams, 78
Cuba, 37, 39
Cuchar, Mike, 33
Culture: deterritorialized, xvii; emergence of hybrid, 81-82; and the ethnic, 19, 32, 77-78; and imperialism, xiii; and primal connection to death, 62; urban, 2. *See also* Architecture; City; Culturescape; Experience; Latino

culture in Manhattan; Popular culture; Punk; Subculture; Technology; Vicariousness
Culturescape, 64-69
Cyborgs, 11-16

Darin, Bobby, 61
de Certeau, Michel, xii
Deleuze, Gilles, xii, xv
del Rio, Dolores, 48
Design, and Greek-column revival fad, 20-21. *See also* Art; Imagery; Kitsch
Dick, Philip K., 12
Diorama, 58-60, 103n.6; the world as, 71
Disease: as metaphor, 98n.16; obsessive compulsive (OCD), 1, 7. *See also* Psychasthenia
Do Androids Dream of Electric Sheep, 12
Docudrama, 10, 98n.15
Dominican Republic, 37
Don Quijote, xix
Duchamp, Marcel 68

Eco, Umberto, xv
Ethnic: as commodity, 19, 32; notion of the, 77-78
Experience: nostalgia, 33-35; waning of affect, 23-24, 40. *See also* Allegory; Anxiety; Benjamin, Walter; Melancholia; Psychasthenia; Vicariousness
Expo '67, 28

Feminism: and the cyborg, 15; and perception of popular culture, xii-xiii; and postmodernism, xiv, 96n.18. *See also* Haraway, Donna; Mesa-Bains, Amalia; Modleski, Tania
Films: Latino culture in, 78-80; and recirculation of B movies, 33; snuff, 10; special-effects, 33; voyeurism in, 98n.13; waning of affect and, 23. *See also*; *Alien; Attack of the 50-foot Woman; Back to the Future; Brazil; Cat Women of the Moon; Crossover Dreams*; del Rio; Docudrama; *The Fly; Forbidden Planet; Full Metal Jacket*; Hollywood; *The Invasion of the Body Snatchers; It! The Terror from Beyond Space; La Bamba; Le Thé au Harem; My Beautiful*

Laundrette; Peggy Sue Got Married;
    Science fiction; Sins of the
    Fleshapoids; The Tingler; Video; The
    War of the Worlds
Flack, Audrey, 49-51, 53
Flaubert, Gustave, 60-61
Florida, 76
Fly, The, 29-30
Forbidden Planet, 29
Fourteenth Street, 36, 43-46. See also
    Little Rickie
Frankenstein, 56, 57
Frankenstein; or The Modern
    Prometheus, 11
Frears, Stephan, 80
From the Pole to the Equator, 70
Full Metal Jacket, 97n.7

García-Canclini, Néstor, xiii
Gianikian, Yervant, 70
Guattari, Félix, xii, xv
Guerreros pacíficos, 88

Habermas, Jürgen, xiv-xv
Hall, Stuart, xvi
Haraway, Donna, xiii, xv, 15-16
Haskin, Byron, 33
Hiller, Susan, 72
Hollywood: and image cults, 48, 89;
    parodied in Brazilian carnival, 83. See
    also Films
Hologram: and aesthetic of urban
    architecture, 2; and fictional cyborg,
    13; urban culture as, 19
Hong Kong, 76
Huysmans, J. K., 60
Huyssen, Andreas, 96nn. 9, 18

Iconography, Catholic religious, and
    kitsch, 36-55. See also Imagery;
    Kitsch
Imagery: colonization of Catholic
    religious, 53-54; in contemporary
    perception xv, 4-5, 64; and image vs.
    icon, 99n.1; recycling of, 64-69. See
    also Iconography; Kitsch; Museums;
    Photography; Still life; United States
Imageworld, 64, 85
INFOQuest, 12
Invasion of the Body Snatchers, The, 30
Isla de Margarita, 76

It! The Terror from Beyond Space, 33

Jameson, Fredric: notion of waning of
    affect, 23-24, 40; on postmodernism
    and capitalism, xvi, 104n.3
Junk art, 67-69
Juran, Nathan, 31

Kahlo, Frida, 48
Kavafy, Konstantin, 60
Kiss of the Spider Woman, The, xiii
Kitsch, 36-55; vs. avant-garde art, 50;
    and postmodernism, xiv, 41; space-
    age, 56; and still life, 73. See also Art
Kubrick, Stanley, 97n.7

La Bamba, 78
Lacan, Jacques, 96n.20, 97n.4
Language: and image, xv, 4-5; use of
    Spanish in America, 77; and use vs.
    exchange value, xvii-xviii
Latin America: and cultural recycling,
    75-91; and immigration to urban
    centers, 53-54. See also Brasília;
    Brazil; Caracas; Carnival; Latino
    culture in Manhattan; Mexico
Latino culture in Manhattan, 37, 46,
    76-80, 82
Le Thé au Harem, 80
Levin, Jennifer, 8-10, 13
Little Rickie, 44-46
London, 80, 88
"Lost in Space," 24
Lower East Side, 36
Lucchi, Angela Ricci, 70
Ludwig, Allan, 61-63
Lyotard, Jean-François, xiv

McLuhan, Marshall, xv
McRobbie, Angela, xii
Madame Bovary, xix
Manaus, 76
Manhattan: homelessness in, 18; night
    clubs in, 37; religious iconography in,
    36-38. See also Canal Street; Casitas;
    Fourteenth Street; Latino culture in
    Manhattan; Little Rickie; Lower East
    Side; Rivington Sculpture Garden;
    Times Square; Upper West Side
Melancholia, 34-35, 57-61, 65. See also

Allegory; Benjamin, Walter;
  Postmodernism
Mesa-Bains, Amalia, 38, 48-49, 53
Mexico, 37, 49. *See also* del Rio; Kahlo,
  Frida; Superbarrio
Miranda, Carmen, 89
Modernism: after the 1950s, xx; and
  space-age fantasy, 35
Modleski, Tania, xii, xiii, xvii
Montreal, 28
Mouffe, Chantal, xvi
Museums: and exhibits on image
  production, 85; public enjoyment of,
  xiii
Music: black urban, xiii; Latin American
  in the U.S., 78-80; punk, 88;
  Spanglish hip hop, 81
My Beautiful Laundrette, 80

Nature morte. *See* Still life
Neumann, Kurt, 29
New York: architecture in, 2; and
  commodification of ruins and decay,
  58; and gangs, 13; Latinization of, 76.
  See also Bronx; Chicano; INFOQuest;
  Kitsch; Manhattan; Nuyorican; Puerto
  Rico; Punk; World's fairs
Nostalgia, 19. *See also* Allegory;
  Benjamin, Walter; Melancholia; Retro
  fashion
Novel. *See Blade Runner, Crash!*
Nuyorican: artists, 53; home altar
  tradition, 47-49; as hybrid culture in
  U.S., 81-82. *See also* Osorio, Pepón;
  Soto, Merián

Obsolescence. *See* Technology
Old Harovian, 59
Organic: body as, 11-12, 23-24; and
  identity, 17-18; revalorization of the,
  69. *See also* Body; Photography; Still
  life
Osorio, Pepón, 81

Paris, 80
Parody: and cultural recycling, 75-76; of
  U.S. image of postcolonial, 82-91.
  See also Science, parody of
Pastiche, 75-76
Peggy Sue Got Married, 30-31

Perception: and the photographic gaze,
  58-60; reformulated, 1-10; and urban
  life, 5, 84-85. *See also* Photography;
  Psychasthenia; Technology;
  Voyeurism
Performance, Latino mixed-media, 81
Photography: of home altars, 49; as
  hunting, 74; and notion of the natural,
  63; and the photographic gaze,
  58-60; recycling of, 70-72; and still
  life, 61-64; of urban decay, 68. *See
  also* Akin, Gwen; Ludwig, Allan;
  Rough Sea project; Sugimoto, Hiroshi;
  Witkin, Joel-Peter
Picasso, Pablo, 53, 68
Popular culture: as object of study, xii-xiii;
  and vicariousness, 40. *See also*
  Breakdancing; Culture; Imagery;
  Kitsch; Latino culture in Manhattan;
  Presley, Elvis; Recycling
Pornography, 5-10
Postmodernism: debate, xi-xxi, 1, 5; and
  feminism, 96n.18; and the grotesque,
  63; and the melancholic sensibility,
  34-35, 64-69; and simulation, 52;
  vicariousness as cultural trait of, 39.
  See also Jameson, Fredric
Presley, Elvis, 36
Progress, architecture and dream of,
  25-26. *See also* Brasília; Space age
Proust, Marcel, 60
Psychasthenia, 1-5, 17-18, 57. *See also*
  Disease; Perception; Space and time
Puerto Rico, 37. *See also Casitas*
Puig, Manuel, xiii
Punk, 86-89; and neo-punk, 32

Rankin, Aimée, 61
Recycling: in advertising, 5-6; in black
  urban music, xiii; of Catholic religious
  imagery, 46-55; of film footage, 33; in
  kitsch, xiv; and postmodernism, xviii;
  Third World cultural, xvi, 75-91. *See
  also* Imagery; Junk art
Referentiality, breakdown of traditional,
  xvi, xviii-xx, 6
Reicheck, Elayne, 70-71
Repetition: in architecture, 2; obsessive
  compulsive, 5-10
Replicants, 11-14. *See also* Body;
  Cyborgs; Experience; Vicariousness

Retro fashion, 19, 23-24, 31-35, 56. *See also* Presley, Elvis
Rio de Janeiro, 83
Rivington Sculpture Garden, 67-68
RoboCop, 12
Rough Sea project, 72
Roussel, Raymond, 60

Salvo, Dana, 49, 53
Sambódromo. *See* Carnival
San Diego. *See* Border Art Workshop
Santiago, 88-89
São Paulo, 25, 85
Scher, Julia, 99n.26
Schwitters, Kurt, 68
Science, parody of, 69-74
Science fiction, xiii, 12-14; and film, 29-31, 33; and space-age fantasy, 24. *See also* Ballard, J. G.; *Blade Runner; Crash!; Do Androids Dream of Electric Sheep*; Replicants; *RoboCop*
Scott, Ridley, 11, 31
Shelley, Mary Wollstonecraft, 11, 56
Sign, 19-22, 39-40; and religious imagery, 46. *See also* Allegory; Imagery; Symbol
Simulation, xix, 5-10, 40, 52, 54, 97n.7. *See also* Baudrillard, Jean
Sins of the Fleshapoids, 33
Smith, Paul: on allegory, 99n.5; on postmodernity, 104n.3
Soto, Leandro, 39
Soto, Merián, 81
Space and time: conflated in postmodern culture, xix, 2-3, 6, 19, 57, 67, 71. *See also* Psychasthenia
Space age: architecture, 24-29; imagery and still life, 73; retro, 19, 23-24, 31-35, 56
Spectator, strategies of multiple, xiii
"Star Trek," 24
Still life, 56-74
Subculture: gang, 13; gay male, 32; neo-punk, 32; yuppie, 32
Sugimoto, Hiroshi, 58-60
Superbarrio, 86-87
Superheroes, as replicants, 12. *See also* Comic books; Replicants; Superbarrio
Surrealism, 53
Surveillance, 13, 15-16, 18, 99n.24. *See also* Scher, Julia

Survival Research Laboratories, 68-69
Symbol: and allegory, 21-24, 34-35, 57-58; and the imaginary, 4-5. *See also* Allegory; Sign

Technology: as destabilizing, xv; fear of, 23-24, 29-31, 34; obsolescence of, 35, 67-69, 93; reformulating contemporary perception, 1-10; in the Third World, xvi; and time, 56-57; and vicariousness, xix. *See also* Cyborgs; Junk art; Photography; Psychasthenia; Replicants; Surveillance; Telecommunications; Television; Video; Voyeurism
Telecommunications, xvi, 39; and AT&T advertising campaign, 12
Television: and fragmentation of the body, 8-10, 13; and space-age retro, 23-24, 33-34. *See also* "Lost in Space"; "Star Trek"
Temptation of Saint Anthony, The, 60
Texas, 76
Times Square, 67
Tingler, The, 33
Tupinicópolis, 82-85

United States: imagery and, xvi, 54; as melting pot, 77-78
Upper West Side, 36

Valdez, Luis, 78
Valens, Ritchie, 78
Venezuela, xvi, 39. *See also* Isla de Margarita
Verhoeven, Paul, 12
Vicariousness, xix, 29-44. *See also* Experience
Video, 6, 92. *See also* Breakdancing; *Guerreros pacificos*
Vietnam War, construction as media spectacle, 97n.7
Violence: and photography, 58-64, 74; and television, 7-10. *See also* Films; Junk art; Science fiction; Surveillance; Survival Research Laboratories; Video; Voyeurism
Voyeurism, 4-13, 17. *See also* Perception; Surveillance; Video

War of the Worlds, The, 33

Warhol, Andy, 52
Washington, D.C., 28
Whitney Museum. *See* Imageworld
Witkin, Joel-Peter, 63-64

Woman as threat, 31, 98n.16. *See also*
    Feminism; Science fiction
World's fairs, xx, 26-29

Zemeckis, Robert, 30

Celeste Olalquiaga was born in Chile and grew up in Caracas and New York City. She received her Ph.D. at Columbia University in 1990 and is now a writer living in New York City.